2021

A BOOK OF
GRACE-FILLED
DAYS

JANE KNUTH

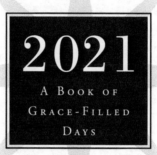

2021

A Book of
Grace-Filled
Days

LOYOLAPRESS.
A JESUIT MINISTRY
Chicago

LOYOLA PRESS.
A JESUIT MINISTRY

3441 N. Ashland Avenue
Chicago, Illinois 60657
(800) 621-1008
www.loyolapress.com

© 2020 Loyola Press
All rights reserved.

Scripture excerpts are taken from the *Lectionary for Mass for Use in the Dioceses of the United States of America, second typical edition*, Copyright 2001, 1998, 1997, 1986, 1970 by the Confraternity of Christian Doctrine, Washington, DC. Used with permission. All rights reserved. No part of the *Lectionary for Mass* may be reproduced in any form without permission in writing from the copyright owner.

Cover and interior design by Kathy Kikkert.

ISBN: 978-0-8294-4888-7
Library of Congress Control Number: 2020935857

Printed in the United States of America.
20 21 22 23 24 25 26 27 28 29 Bang 10 9 8 7 6 5 4 3 2 1

INTRODUCTION

Before beginning this project, I asked my daughter how she viewed "reflections on Scripture." She said, "Well, most of the time when people want a reflection, they go to a mirror."

My hope is that you find in these pages small, reflected glimpses of yourself. And of God.

At the end of writing the book, after spending nine months of daily reflections, out of curiosity I took a tally of the main themes that kept returning in the manuscript. What had the Bible been saying to my heart during all those weeks and months? The number-one idea that repeated itself fifty-seven times over the year was *God is present: believe it.*

That was unexpected.

I kind of thought the themes of love or mercy would completely dominate, but they came in second (forty-nine). I learned something about myself and about my relationship with God. Maybe my need to believe in God's presence has something to do with why I frequently go to daily Mass? Or . . . could it be that God needs me to believe in God's presence?

Do you see how reflecting on Scripture may help you learn about yourself and God, too?

Here's a different idea—but some of you may like it: As you go through the year, dog-ear the pages that touch your heart—the ones that make you say, "Uh-oh." Then, at the end of the book, go back and tally up the main themes from your tagged pages. Here are some of the ones I tagged: joy, hope, obedience or service, fear, control, judgment, connection, searching or stretching, paradox, mystery or uncertainty, humility, power, simplicity, truth, creativity, prayer, unity or connection, and the poor.

Like me, you may be startled by which Scripture themes spoke to you the loudest and most often. Next year at this time, that may be the best Christmas gift you receive.

Meanwhile, may God bless you and keep you. Always. He is present.

Jane

May he not come suddenly and find you sleeping.
—MARK 13:36

Actually, I kind of envy people who die in their sleep. God comes in the night and whisks them away. No time spent on tearful goodbyes, struggling last breaths, or terrified confessions. Perhaps people who die in their sleep are ready to meet God? Maybe each day they make amends with neighbors, say, "I love you" to relatives and children, and are humbled by pain, illness, or failure. Getting ready for the holidays is not the same as getting ready to meet God. Polishing the wine glasses, wrapping the gifts, baking the cookies, and sending cards have all become ways for me to create the perfect celebration. But if the house is all decorated, then I am not ready: *my house* is ready. Getting myself ready to meet God is what Advent is about. My soul is God's house.

Isaiah 63:16b–17,19b; 64:2–7
Psalm 80:2–3,15–16,18–19(4)
1 Corinthians 1:3–9
Mark 13:33–37

⇒ 1 ⇐

NOVEMBER 30

• ST. ANDREW, APOSTLE •

And how can they believe in him
of whom they have not heard?
And how can they hear without someone to preach?
And how can people preach unless they are sent?
—ROMANS 10:14–15

Anyone holding this little book has heard of Jesus. Let us assume that we are either a believer or on the way to becoming one and that we have heard some preaching about Jesus as well. The first two lines of verse above are taken care of. It's that third line that feels awkward. Make no mistake: if we persist along these lines, we will be sent. And after the sending comes the preaching. Paul lays out the process clearly. Don't stress; joy comes from all this. Today, my heart says, "Dear St. Andrew, you who were sent by Jesus, please, pray for me."

Romans 10:9–18
Psalm 19:8,9,10,11
Matthew 4:18–22

DECEMBER 1

There shall be no harm or ruin on all my holy mountain;
for the earth shall be filled with knowledge
of the LORD,
as water covers the sea.
—ISAIAH 11:9

The reading from Isaiah is beautiful. It's a vision of things as
we long for them to be. The vision is a glimpse of God's
"holy mountain," where nothing is destroyed or ruined. A
place covered with "knowledge of the LORD." Perhaps
knowledge of the Lord is what we need to keep from ruining
ourselves and our world. If we really "see" God and "hear" the
words of his Son, we will not feel compelled to harm
ourselves and destroy the planet. If we love God, we will be
able to love anything and everything that God loves. That is
a beautiful vision to reach for.

Isaiah 11:1–10
Psalm 72:1–2,7–8,12–13,17
Luke 10:21–24

Wednesday

DECEMBER 2

The LORD of hosts
will provide for all peoples
a feast of rich food and choice wines.
—ISAIAH 25:6

All three readings tell how God will feed his people lavishly.
This is nice, but today we know that nearly 12 percent of
households in the United States have food insecurity issues
(USDA, 2017 Food Security Status). In the Society of
St. Vincent de Paul, we have studied how different economic
groups view meals. The rich are mostly concerned with
whether the presentation of the food is right: Are the candles
lit, is the silver polished, is the food special? The reading
from Isaiah talks about this. The middle class values tasty
food: my grandmother's recipe, whipped cream on top, and a
variety of dishes: "You spread the table before me"
(Psalm 23:5). The poor ask this: Was there enough for
everybody, did you eat your fill? Jesus had seven baskets of
leftovers (Matthew 15:37).

Isaiah 25:6–10a
Psalm 23:1–3a,3b–4,5,6
Matthew 15:29–37

DECEMBER 3

• ST. FRANCIS XAVIER, PRIEST •

*"The rain fell, the floods came,
and the winds blew and buffeted the house.
And it collapsed and was completely ruined."*
—MATTHEW 7:27

God is not trying to save my house. He is not trying to save my country, either. He is not interested in my preferred political system or in the health of the economy. God is not trying to save my church denomination or any of the church buildings. He has no need for the educational institutions, and he can let our entertainment venues disappear in the blink of an eye. God only wants to save my soul. He wants to save me from pride, from greed, from lust, from hatred, and from despair. It is foolishness to put my faith in anyone or anything except God and what he wants.

Isaiah 26:1–6
Psalm 118:1 and 8–9,19–21,25–27a
Matthew 7:21,24–27

DECEMBER 4

• ST. JOHN DAMASCENE, PRIEST AND DOCTOR OF THE CHURCH •

> *Then he touched their eyes and said,*
> *"Let it be done for you according to your faith."*
> *And their eyes were opened.*
> —MATTHEW 9:29–30

A joyful YouTube video at https://www.youtube.com/watch?v=2hf3Br_32kY shows color-blind people trying on sunglasses that allow them to see in color. They stare at the eyes of their children and see blue for the first time. They walk from flower to flower in the garden, exclaiming in wonder. One of them says in awe, "Is this purple? And that's blue? The leaves are different from the trees! Oh, my God, it's beautiful!" When Jesus gave sight to the two blind men, imagine what they said: "Is that a tree? Does everyone look different from one another? Is the sky always blue? Oh, my God, it's so beautiful!" Jesus gave them joy. He wants that joy for me, as well. He wants me to truly see.

Isaiah 29:17–24
Psalm 27:1,4,13–14
Matthew 9:27–31

DECEMBER 5

The LORD rebuilds Jerusalem;
the dispersed of Israel he gathers.
He heals the brokenhearted
and binds up their wounds.
—PSALM 147:2–3

I am writing this in December of 2018, and there are broken
hearts and wounded people all around me. God did not
prevent these hearts from breaking, and none of us walks
through life without getting wounded. He doesn't promise
safety from injury or absence of sorrow. He promises healing.
Jesus walked around Galilee healing people. Then he sent
out the disciples and gave them power to do the same. In
2021, I suspect that there will be plenty of healing needed as
well. I am not a counselor or a doctor. But I can heal by
encouraging the discouraged, by feeding the hungry, by
taking a load off weary shoulders, and by offering a tender
compassionate look. The Lord rebuilds Jerusalem with my
hands and gathers the dispersed with my welcome.

Isaiah 30:19–21,23–26
Psalm 147:1–2,3–4,5–6
Matthew 9:35—10:1,5a,6–8

Sunday

DECEMBER 6

• SECOND SUNDAY OF ADVENT •

John the Baptist appeared in the desert
proclaiming a baptism of repentance for the forgiveness
of sins.
People of the Judean countryside
and all the inhabitants of Jerusalem
were going out to him
and were being baptized by him in the Jordan River
as they acknowledged their sins.
—MARK 1:4–5

I am trying to imagine that a preacher appears in the farmland around my town, announcing that we are sinners and we need to repent. Would I even drive out there and listen to him speak? No. If he was asking people to walk into the river, would I cringe? Yes. If a trusted friend asked me to go listen, would I? Perhaps, if I wasn't busy. John the Baptist is too intense for me. I prefer my preachers in pressed robes, telling me that I am doing well. It is a long way to Bethlehem from where I am.

Isaiah 40:1–5,9–11
Psalm 85:9–10,11–12,13–14(8)
2 Peter 3:8–14
Mark 1:1–8

───────────

⇒ 8 ⇐

"Which is easier, to say, 'Your sins are forgiven,'
or to say, 'Rise and walk'?"
—LUKE 5:23

Which is easier for me to hear? I am one of those "roll up
your sleeves and get working" kind of Christians. I would
rather serve at a soup kitchen than go to confession. I would
rather hear Jesus say to me, "Get up and get going" instead
of, "Don't worry about it; I've forgiven you." The first makes
me feel needed. The second makes me cry and feel needy. I
guess I don't want to need God; I would prefer that God
need me. But all I ever get from self-sufficiency is anxiety and
pride. Deep in my heart, I know that peace comes from
needing God.

Isaiah 35:1–10
Psalm 85:9ab and 10,11–12,13–14
Luke 5:17–26

• THE IMMACULATE CONCEPTION OF THE BLESSED VIRGIN MARY
(PATRONAL FEAST DAY OF THE UNITED STATES OF AMERICA) •

Mary said, "Behold, I am the handmaid of the Lord.
May it be done to me according to your word."
—LUKE 1:38

Mary did not say, "I've got this. How hard can it be? When do I start?" Nope. She said, "May it be done to me according to your word." This is not a show of self-confidence. This is the kind of humility that realizes that nothing is going as she planned but that God will do everything to her. Okay, then let it be done. Wouldn't it be amazing if we could begin each day that way? We climb out of bed and say, "God, whatever you do to me today, let it be so."

Genesis 3:9–15,20
Psalm 98:1,2–3ab,3cd–4
Ephesians 1:3–6,11–12
Luke 1:26–38

DECEMBER 9

• ST. JUAN DIEGO CUAUHTLATOATZIN •

Jesus said to the crowds:
"Come to me, all you who labor and are burdened,
and I will give you rest."
—MATTHEW 11:28

Where did we ever get the idea that God wants us to work harder? We think he wants us to volunteer more, be more diligent in our jobs, persevere past the point of exhaustion, and pray longer. Jesus does not exhort his followers to work harder. He knows we have enough work to do already. Sometimes, he asks us to pray for more workers, but never for more work. "God helps those who help themselves" is not in the Bible. "Come to me . . . and I will give you rest" is in the Bible.

Isaiah 40:25–31
Psalm 103:1–2,3–4,8 and 10
Matthew 11:28–30

I am the LORD, your God,
who grasp your right hand;
It is I that say to you, Fear not,
I will help you.
—ISAIAH 41:13

I try to practice being aware of the presence of God, but whenever I get busy or distracted, I forget. I start out the day telling myself, "God is here, God is here, God is here," and then back my car down the driveway and completely forget his name. Until I get in trouble or become afraid—then I remember God again. This verse from Isaiah says that God grasps my right hand. I don't have to remember to reach for his—he has already grabbed hold of mine. He really is a good father.

Isaiah 41:13–20
Psalm 145:1 and 9,10–11,12–13ab
Matthew 11:11–15

DECEMBER 11

Jesus said to the crowds: . . .
"For John came neither eating nor drinking,
and they said,
'He is possessed by a demon.'
The Son of Man came eating and drinking
and they said,
'Look, he is a glutton and a drunkard.'"
—MATTHEW 11:18–19

I think what Jesus is saying is, *people are complicated.* I say this to myself whenever I run across baffling opinions, reactions, or illogic. It makes me less judgmental than if I say, "Those people are absurd, stupid, misinformed, or evil." I need a lot of practice being less judgmental, so this is a good phrase for me. It keeps me calm.

Isaiah 48:17–19
Psalm 1:1–2,3,4,6
Matthew 11:16–19

Saturday

DECEMBER 12

• OUR LADY OF GUADALUPE •

"Your deed of hope will never be forgotten
by those who tell of the might of God."
—JUDITH 13:19

The story of Our Lady of Guadalupe has everything to make
my heart soar: a poor, afflicted man, a beautiful apparition of
Mary, disbelief by the higher-ups, miraculous roses, and an
icon that has lasted way beyond anyone's expectations. It's no
wonder that strong men get her image tattooed on their
arms. It is a story of hope—hope that "will never be
forgotten by those who tell of the might of God."

Zechariah 2:14–17 or Revelation 11:19a; 12:1–6a,10ab
Judith 13:18bcde,19
Luke 1:26–38 or 1:39–47

Some Pharisees were also sent.
They asked him,
"Why then do you baptize
if you are not the Christ, or Elijah, or the Prophet?"
—JOHN 1:24–25

The Pharisees do not like what John the Baptist is doing. He is inspiring people to change. He is condemning the misuses of power. He is attracting crowds outside of controlled venues. The Pharisees have a little bit of power, and they are feeling threatened by John, who has no worldly power at all. Perhaps they know that God sends the powerless. Paul writes in Thessalonians 5:19–20: "Do not quench the Spirit. Do not despise prophetic utterances." Paul knows that God sends the powerless, and he is warning us not to silence them. Who are the powerless people who threaten me?

Isaiah 61:1–2a,10–11
Luke 1:46–48,49–50,53–54
1 Thessalonians 5:16–24
John 1:6–8,19–28

The chief priests and the elders of the people approached him as he was teaching and said, "By what authority are you doing these things?" . . . Jesus said to them in reply, "I shall ask you one question, and if you answer it for me, then I shall tell you by what authority I do these things. Where was John's baptism from? Was it of heavenly or of human origin?" . . . So they said to Jesus in reply, "We do not know." He himself said to them, "Neither shall I tell you by what authority I do these things."

—MATTHEW 21:23–25,27

In a way, the chief priests and the elders are asking Jesus to provide his credentials for teaching in the temple. He, in turn, asks them if John the Baptist had the right credentials. They claim ignorance. Jesus leaves them in their ignorance.

Numbers 24:2–7,15–17a
Psalm 25:4–5ab,6 and 7bc,8–9
Matthew 21:23–27

DECEMBER 15

*Jesus said to them, "Amen, I say to you,
tax collectors and prostitutes
are entering the Kingdom of God before you."*
—MATTHEW 21:31

Whenever I hear people gripe about the IRS, I think of this statement of Jesus. When government bureaucrats look to God, the Almighty welcomes them into his kingdom. Jesus loves the accountants who collect our taxes no matter how much the rest of society derides them. It was not chance that made him choose St. Matthew as one of his apostles.

Whenever the subject of prostitution comes up, I think of the great mercy of God. God has pity for people who are forced to make a living by selling their bodies. We condemn their actions, but we cannot see their hearts. Jesus sees their hearts: "He said to the woman, 'Your faith has saved you; go in peace'" (Luke 7:50).

Zephaniah 3:1–2,9–13
Psalm 34:2–3,6–7,17–18,19 and 23
Matthew 21:28–32

DECEMBER 16

"Go and tell John what you have seen and heard:
the blind regain their sight,
the lame walk,
lepers are cleansed,
the deaf hear, the dead are raised,
the poor have the good news proclaimed to them."
—LUKE 7:22

My parents weren't into Santa. They played along with the story, but they emphasized baby Jesus more. When I was six, I heard rumors at school, so I went to my mom and asked, "Are you Santa? Do you put the gifts under the tree?" She smiled softly and said, "Let's keep that secret between you and me. We don't want to spoil it for your little sisters." I nodded, honored to be part of my mom's secret. Then, thinking a minute, I asked, "Do the older kids know?" Mom smiled again. I think John knew who Jesus was. He sent his disciples to find out for themselves.

Isaiah 45:6c–8,18,21c–25
Psalm 85:9ab and 10,11–12,13–14
Luke 7:18b–23

DECEMBER 17

Jacob the father of Joseph, the husband of Mary.
Of her was born Jesus.
—MATTHEW 1:16

Notice that Matthew names a bunch of ancestors of Jesus *through Joseph's line.* But Mary gave birth to Jesus as a virgin, so what does it matter who Joseph's relatives were?

It matters because adoption is legitimate. Adoptive parents are parents. Adoptive grandparents are grandparents. My maiden name is Hudson, and my brother did some genealogy research tracking our family back to the 1700s. Then he submitted a sample to a DNA-tracking firm. Curiously, we are not genetically related to any other people named Hudson. And the more curious thing is that we *are related to lots and lots of people named Streeter.* Furthermore, in the census files back in the early 1800s, he found that Streeter was the name of my great-great-grandparents' neighbors. Hmm? This is hilarious. But we are still Hudsons.

Genesis 49:2,8–10
Psalm 72:1–2,3–4ab,7–8,17
Matthew 1:1–17

"Joseph, son of David,
do not be afraid to take Mary your wife
into your home."
—MATTHEW 1:20

So, why was Joseph "afraid" to take Mary into his home?
Talk. People talk. Joseph had a reputation as a just man.
Maybe he was afraid of losing the esteem of his small town,
afraid of the cruelty of town gossip. I'm pretty sure the gossip
happened even after he brought Mary to live with him.
People can count nine months on their fingers. How much
harm I do by criticizing people! My critical spirit is
something that I need to lose this Advent season.

Jeremiah 23:5–8
Psalm 72:1–2,12–13,18–19
Matthew 1:18–25

DECEMBER 19

His wife was barren and had borne no children.
—JUDGES 13:2

But they had no child, because Elizabeth was barren.
—LUKE 1:7

Today we read stories about two barren women being told that they will conceive. In the book of Judges, it is Samson's mother. An angel visits her, announces the coming child, and then she tells her husband. In Matthew, Zechariah is visited by the angel. He can only make hand signals because he is struck mute for his disbelief. I wonder how he told Elizabeth that they were going to have a baby? She must have figured out the hand signals, and she must have believed, because she wasn't struck dumb. When it appears that God is doing something wonderful in my life, it is wise to believe it is God.

Judges 13:2–7,24–25a
Psalm 71:3–4a,5–6ab,16–17
Luke 1:5–25

DECEMBER 20

*"Go, tell my servant David, 'Thus says the LORD:
Should you build me a house to dwell in?'"*
—2 SAMUEL 7:5

God wants to dwell in our hearts. God is not interested in buildings. In the years just before the time of the Protestant Reformation, the Catholic Church was building St. Peter's Basilica in Rome. It cost a lot of money, so one of the ways they financed it was by selling indulgences. People who had sinned could purchase an indulgence for the forgiveness of their waywardness. Martin Luther was famously not happy about this clear advantage for the rich over the poor. He was correct. It was wrong. But what we often forget is that it all came about because of a big building project. God wants to dwell in our hearts, not in our buildings. First things first.

2 Samuel 7:1–5,8b–12,14a,16
Psalm 89:2–3,4–5,27,29(2a)
Romans 16:25–27
Luke 1:26–38

"And how does this happen to me,
that the mother of my Lord should come to me?"
—LUKE 1:43

Elizabeth is a relative of Mary, and she is surprised and delighted to have her visit. We are not relatives of Mary, and we doubt that she would visit us. *But she comes.* In the last two centuries she has come more than we could ask or imagine. St. Catherine Laboure received the Miraculous Medal from Mary in 1830. She appeared to two children in LaSalette, France, in 1846. Twelve years later, she came to Lourdes and spoke with St. Bernadette. Then, in 1871, Pontmain, France; 1879, Knock, Ireland; 1917, Fatima, Portugal; 1968, Cairo, Egypt; 1973, Akita, Japan; 1976, Betania, Venezuela; and 1981, Kibeho, Rwanda. These are some approved by the Church. There are many more still under investigation such as Medjugorje, Bosnia. Open your door—*she comes!*

Song of Songs 2:8–14, or Zephaniah 3:14–18a
Psalm 33:2–3,11–12,20–21
Luke 1:39–45

DECEMBER 22

Mary said:
"My soul proclaims the greatness of the Lord;
my spirit rejoices in God my savior,
for he has looked upon his lowly servant.
From this day all generations will call me blessed:
the Almighty has done great things for me,
and holy is his Name.
He has mercy on those who fear him
in every generation."
—LUKE 1:46–50

In Mary's Canticle, in five verses she expresses praise, joy, humility, prophecy, spiritual intimacy, and God's providence and mercy. Go ahead and read it again, and you'll see. She has a way of understanding the essentials. Ask her to help you do the same.

1 Samuel 1:24–28
1 Samuel 2:1,4–5,6–7,8abcd
Luke 1:46–56

DECEMBER 23

• ST. JOHN OF KANTY, PRIEST •

Lo, I am sending my messenger
to prepare the way before me.
—MALACHI 3:1

Why does God need a messenger to prepare the way for
God? Why doesn't God do that? I don't know the answer to
this question, but this precursor business seems to be the way
God works. That's what prophets are for. My friend Peggy
once said to me, "We ought to all be praying for the gift of
prophecy." I was shocked. Who in their right mind would
want to be a prophet? Look what happened to them! John
the Baptist is an excellent example of someone who did
exactly what God asked of him. I have a hard time praying
for the gift of prophecy. There must be someone else who
would like the job more than I would.

Malachi 3:1–4,23–24
Psalm 25:4–5ab,8–9,10 and 14
Luke 1:57–66

DECEMBER 24

*To shine on those who dwell in darkness
and the shadow of death,
and to guide our feet into the way of peace.*
—LUKE 1:79

The day before Christmas has never been a peaceful day for me. Growing up in a family of eight children, I experienced it as a day filled with cleaning, last-minute baking and wrapping, and an anxious mother. Despite the tumult of the day, the anticipation of Christmas was so intense that the stress seemed normal. Even today, I still jump out of bed on December 24, my mind whirling with all that has to get done and all the excitement of the holiday. It's a type of darkness, this stress. I know better than to get myself all worked up, but I do it anyway. This is the first Christmas since my mom's passing. I wonder if I can let "death's shadow" leave me and let peace lead me.

2 Samuel 7:1–5,8b–12,14a,16
Psalm 89:2–3,4–5,27 and 29
Luke 1:67–79

DECEMBER 25

*She wrapped him in swaddling clothes and laid him
in a manger,
because there was no room for them in the inn.*
—LUKE 2:7

Can you imagine this? Giving birth in a barn and putting that
newborn baby in the feed trough? Near the end of my
pregnancies, I got what they call a "nesting instinct," obsessed
with painting rooms, cleaning closets, getting meals into the
freezer, and packing my hospital bag. I drove my husband to
distraction. He didn't understand why everything had to be
ready ahead of time. But my maternal soul cried out, "Get
ready!" I shudder thinking about Mary giving birth this way.
All she had were some swaddling clothes. And her heart.

VIGIL:	DAWN:
Isaiah 62:1–5	Isaiah 62:11–12
Psalm 89:4–5,16–17,27,29(2a)	Psalm 97:1,6,11–12
Acts 13:16–17,22–25	Titus 3:4–7
Matthew 1:1–25 or 1:18–25	Luke 2:15–20

NIGHT:	DAY:
Isaiah 9:1–6	Isaiah 52:7–10
Psalm 96:1–2,2–3,11–12,13	Psalm 98:1,2–3,3–4,5–6(3c)
Titus 2:11–14	Hebrews 1:1–6
Luke 2:1–14	John 1:1–18 or 1:1–5,9–14

They threw him out of the city, and began to stone him.
—ACTS 7:58

Stephen was stoned for heresy, for claiming that Jesus was the Messiah. Juris Rubenis, a Latvian pastor, once wrote, "A religion is alive when it has a lot of unburned heretics." I think he is saying that it is a sign of a dead religion when everyone agrees, when the heretics have all been excommunicated, burned, or stoned. A heretic is not necessarily a schismatic. Jesus ordered us to love everybody. He was crucified for heresy. In order to keep Catholicism alive, it's essential that we love our heretics and keep them.

Acts 6:8–10; 7:54–59
Psalm 31:3cd–4,6 and 8ab,16bc and 17
Matthew 10:17–22

Sunday
DECEMBER 27

• THE HOLY FAMILY OF JESUS, MARY, AND JOSEPH •

The child grew and became strong, filled with wisdom;
and the favor of God was upon him.
—LUKE 2:40

On the Feast of the Holy Family, we read about how the
child Jesus grew strong, wise, and close to God. That strikes
me as the perfect prayer for parents to say over their
children: "Please, God, make our kids strong, wise, and let
them know you." What else could we want as parents? We
don't mean to encourage our kids to be popular, overly
competitive, greedy, perfectionistic, sly, or deceptive, but the
culture often pushes them in those directions. Even though
our daughters are in their thirties, we still pray for them each
day, and we often ask for strength, wisdom, and faith.

Genesis 15:1–6, 21:1–3 or Sirach 3:2–6,12–14
Psalm 105:1–2,3–4,5–6,8–9(7a,8a) or Psalm 128:1–2,3,4–5 or 3:12–17
Hebrews 11:8,11–12,17–19 or Colossians 3:12–21 or 3:12–17
Luke 2:22–40 or 2:22,39–40 or 3:12–17

*Joseph rose and took the child and his mother by night
and departed for Egypt.*
—MATTHEW 2:14

Under the influence of a warning in a dream, Joseph got up,
acted quickly, and fled. Joseph is the hero in this story.
Sometimes, I wonder if all the young fathers in Bethlehem
were given the same bad dream but shook it off and went
back to sleep? I don't think Joseph was an anxious worrier; he
always seemed to be able to sleep, anyway. But when he was
given a warning, he didn't shrug it off. In my life, even when
things look really bad, I am the one who says, "Let's go to
sleep and deal with it in the morning." Joseph went to sleep,
but he got up in the night.

1 John 1:5—2:2
Psalm 124:2–3,4–5,7b–8
Matthew 2:13–18

DECEMBER 29

• ST. THOMAS BECKET, BISHOP AND MARTYR •

Whoever loves his brother remains in the light,
and there is nothing in him to cause a fall.
Whoever hates his brother is in darkness;
he walks in darkness
and does not know where he is going
because the darkness has blinded his eyes.
—1 JOHN 2:10–11

When someone on television, on the Internet, or in my own living room speaks about another person with contempt, derision, or hatred, I stop listening. "Whoever hates his brother is in darkness . . . and does not know where he is going." Why listen to people who don't know where they are going? And on the other hand, when someone speaks lovingly of people, refrains from derision even when it is deserved, or refuses to fear "the other," I sit up and listen carefully. I want to share in their light.

1 John 2:3–11
Psalm 96:1–2a,2b–3,5b–6
Luke 2:22–35

DECEMBER 30

Do not love the world or the things of the world.
If anyone loves the world, the love of the Father
is not in him.
—1 JOHN 2:15

Here we are, just coming off Christmas, and this reading pops up. The "things of the world" are still sitting in their boxes underneath my Christmas tree. I love the Christmas season: the carols, the gifts, the parties, the extravagant meals, the excited children, and the nostalgia of holiday traditions. There is nothing wrong or evil about these things; they just are not what I am supposed to love. I am supposed to love the coming of the Divine into a human body so that we will know how loved we are. And I do love that. Help me, Father, to love you more than your world. Amen.

1 John 2:12–17
Psalm 96:7–8a,8b–9,10
Luke 2:36–40

Thursday

DECEMBER 31

• ST. SYLVESTER I, POPE •

Let the heavens be glad and the earth rejoice;
let the sea and what fills it resound;
let the plains be joyful and all that is in them.
Then shall all the trees of the forest exult before the LORD.
—PSALM 96:11–12

The image of trees rejoicing is one of those splendidly quirky
phrases that remind me of children's literature.
Anthropomorphizing the trees, the plains, the sea, the
heavens, and the earth delights me. It makes me want to
paint a forest of trees with faces, an ocean with bugle-playing
porpoises, and stars with eyes. It's the kind of illustration that
can be found only in board books. It is certain that God is
head-over-heels in love with children, because Psalm 96 is
written for children and for the childlike.

1 John 2:18–21
Psalm 96:1–2,11–12,13
John 1:1–18

JANUARY 1

All who heard it were amazed
by what had been told them by the shepherds.
—LUKE 2:18

God chose shepherds to be the first eyewitnesses of his incarnation. Who are the shepherds of today? Who works in the fields? Migrant laborers. Who smells of animals and dung? Slaughterhouse workers. Who stays up all night protecting property? Security guards and desk clerks. God may choose these same people to herald his second coming. If somebody dressed in Carhartts tells me that Jesus has returned, will I smile and walk away? And if a security guard claims he heard music coming from the sky, will I go outside to check it out? If a night desk clerk tells me about seeing angels, will I pause to listen to her story? Will I allow myself to be amazed?

Numbers 6:22–27
Psalm 67:2–3,5,6,8(2a)
Galatians 4:4–7
Luke 2:16–21

Saturday

JANUARY 2

And this is the promise that he made us: eternal life.
—1 JOHN 2:25

Eternal life means that we live forever. Jesus promised that
our essence will not die even when our bodies die. Then he
proved this by walking the earth after he was brutally killed
in front of the entire town and buried. He did all he could to
convince us that we are eternal creatures, and for good
reason: believing in our own immortality is power,
responsibility, and joy.

1 John 2:22–28
Psalm 98:1,2–3ab,3cd–4
John 1:19–28

*That the Gentiles are coheirs, members of the
same Body,
and copartners in the promise in Christ Jesus
through the gospel.*
—EPHESIANS 3:6

Who are these Gentiles? In biblical times, they were
everybody who wasn't a Jew: the Greeks, the Egyptians, the
Philistines, all the neighboring nations, and even the
despised Romans who were occupying their land. Who are
the Gentiles today? The biker with the crucifix tattoo? The
girl with the rosary beads hanging from her rearview mirror
who just cut me off on the freeway? The alcoholic sleeping
in the vacant doorway? The lady scolding me because I have
too many items in the express checkout? The politician who
voted to raise my taxes? The immigrants? Who are my
coheirs? This is not an easy teaching.

Isaiah 60:1–6
Psalm 72:1–2,7–8,10–11,12–13
Ephesians 3:2–3a,5–6
Matthew 2:1–12

And his commandment is this:
we should believe in the name of his Son,
Jesus Christ,
and love one another just as he commanded us.
—1 JOHN 3:23

This is clear and simple: believe in Jesus and love one another. But then the writer goes on to describe how to tell if a spirit is from God or from the antichrist, who "in fact is already in the world." So, maybe it's not so simple? Apparently, testing the spirits involves finding out if the spirit acknowledges Jesus. But just saying the name of Jesus isn't proof. All kinds of people talk about Jesus. I think the second half of the Scripture quotation is the most reliable way to test the spirit: "and love one another just as he commanded." If I talk about Jesus but don't love people, I am not to be trusted.

1 John 3:22—4:6
Psalm 2:7bc–8,10–12a
Matthew 4:12–17,23–25

*He said to them in reply,
"Give them some food yourselves."
But they said to him,
"Are we to buy two hundred days' wages
worth of food
and give it to them to eat?"*
—MARK 6:37

Jesus says this to me *All. The. Time.* Mostly I ignore him.
St. Jude's hospital sends me letters asking for contributions;
the local food pantry always wants peanut butter and tuna;
the St. Vincent de Paul Society, the Red Cross, the Salvation
Army, the Bishop, and the guy with the piece of cardboard at
the end of the freeway ramp. I—same as the apostles—roll
my eyes and say to Jesus, "How do you expect me to feed all
these people?" He just grins. On those occasions when I
don't ignore Jesus, the miracles happen after I do what he
asks, not before.

1 John 4:7–10
Psalm 72:1–2,3–4,7–8
Mark 6:34–44

JANUARY 6

• ST. ANDRÉ BESSETTE, RELIGIOUS •

He got into the boat with them and the wind died down.
They were completely astounded.
They had not understood the incident of the loaves.
On the contrary, their hearts were hardened.
—MARK 6:51–52

One miracle is never enough. Two miracles are seldom sufficient either. We think that God doesn't want to help us and that we need to work hard and earn our good fortune. This is what it means to have a hard heart. I have heard it said that superstition grows in a society when faith in God wanes. Our society believes in lottery tickets, casinos, or the stock market. Our hearts are not soft enough to cry out to God every time the seas rise or the winds blow. We are astonished when we are rescued once and can't believe that it will happen again. One miracle is never enough. God keeps trying. Google André Bessette.

1 John 4:11–18
Psalm 72:1–2,10,12–13
Mark 6:45–52

JANUARY 7

• ST. RAYMOND OF PENYAFORT, PRIEST •

"The Spirit of the Lord is upon me,
because he has anointed me
to bring glad tidings to the poor."
—LUKE 4:18

Sometimes I make following Jesus too complicated. He
simplifies it with this statement.

1 John 4:19—5:4
Psalm 72:1–2,14 and 15bc,17
Luke 4:14–22

Jesus stretched out his hand, touched him, and said,
"I do will it. Be made clean."
And the leprosy left him immediately.
—LUKE 5:13

Such a bold prayer: "Lord, if you want to, you can heal me."
Jesus wanted to heal the leper, so he did it. This story makes
me wonder how many times I have been healed. That allergy
that the doctor said I "grew out of." The knee that made me
limp for a year, then stopped hurting and never needed
surgery after all. The anxiety that made me slow down,
exercise, eat right—and then gradually went away. Perhaps,
when I prayed, Jesus stretched out his hand and said, "I do
will it."

1 John 5:5–13
Psalm 147:12–13,14–15,19–20
Luke 5:12–16

Saturday

JANUARY 9

"So this joy of mine has been made complete.
He must increase; I must decrease."
—JOHN 3:29–30

I am searching for joy. Who is not? If I am to become one
with Christ, if I am to join the communion of saints in
heaven, if I am to be the face of Christ to the poor, and if I
am to decrease while Christ increases, then I must pray for
the humility of John the Baptist. He understood that his
mission was to reveal the Christ, not run the show. Humility
does not say, "I am a worm." Humility recognizes who we are
as God's children on the earth and recognizes who we are
not, as well. John the Baptist, the greatest of prophets, said
he was not the Messiah, and he also said, "This joy of mine
has been made complete."

1 John 5:14–21
Psalm 149:1–2,3–4,5 and 6a and 9b
John 3:22–30

JANUARY 10

• THE BAPTISM OF THE LORD •

Seek the LORD while he may be found,
call him while he is near.
—ISAIAH 55:6

We know that the Lord is always near, that God desires to be
found. But Isaiah hints that there may come a time when this
is not so. Our hearts can become so hardened that we no
longer search for God. Our ego becomes so big that God's
nearness is meaningless. We raise our voices, and God's small,
quiet voice cannot be heard. We use our weapons, our
money, our influence, our deceptions, and we tell God to
step aside while we fix matters in our own way. God is near.
He is at the river being baptized. He is walking our streets
dressed in old clothes. He is blessing us with his tears as we
die. He is not holding the weapons or the money. He is
holding joy.

Isaiah 42:1–4,6–7 or 55:1–11
Psalm 29:1–2,3–4,3,9–10 or Isaiah 12:2–3,4bcd,5–6
Acts 10:34–38 or 1 John 5:1–9
Mark 1:7–11

Jesus came to Galilee proclaiming the Gospel of God:
"This is the time of fulfillment.
The Kingdom of God is at hand.
Repent, and believe in the Gospel."
—MARK 1:14–15

If Jesus came to your house, sat down in front of you, and said, "Repent, and believe in the Gospel," what would you do? Close your eyes and picture him in front of you. This may take a little time. Now, take a pen and paper and write 1, 2, 3 in a column. Close your eyes. Ask Jesus what you need to repent of. Write it next to number one. Close your eyes again. Ask Jesus what you need to believe. Write it next to number two. Close your eyes again. Ask Jesus to bring his kingdom into your heart by helping you begin to forgive someone. Write the person's initials. The kingdom of God is at hand.

Hebrews 1:1–6
Psalm 97:1 and 2b,6 and 7c,9
Mark 1:14–20

The people were astonished at his teaching,
for he taught them as one having authority
and not as the scribes.
—MARK 1:22

While pondering this Bible verse, I asked myself if I had ever been "astonished" at someone's teaching about God. My conclusion was yes. St. Vincent de Paul taught that the poor are our lords and masters because Christ is in the poor, and we should treat them as such. I had been assisting people in poverty for many years, but the idea that I was their servant and should drop everything at their command left me dumbfounded. I was truly astonished that charitable work is not something I volunteer to do; it is something I am commanded to do. I am commanded by my lord and master, Jesus Christ, who lives in the poor. Have you ever been astonished by someone's teaching?

Hebrews 2:5–12
Psalm 8:2ab and 5,6–7,8–9
Mark 1:21–28

*Simon and those who were with him pursued him
and on finding him said, "Everyone is looking
for you."
He told them, "Let us go on to the nearby villages
that I may preach there also.
For this purpose have I come."*
—MARK 1:36–38

Oh, how I wish that everyone today were looking for Jesus.
Wouldn't that be amazing? Maybe the problem is that too
many people stop looking when they think they have him in
their town already. Is that why he has to keep moving to
other towns all the time? So that we keep looking?

Hebrews 2:14–18
Psalm 105:1–2,3–4,6–7,8–9
Mark 1:29–39

Thursday

JANUARY 14

*The leprosy left him immediately, and he was
made clean.
Then, warning him sternly, he dismissed him at once.
Then he said to him, "See that you tell no one anything. . . ."
The man went away and began to publicize
the whole matter . . .
so that it was impossible for Jesus to enter a town openly.*
—MARK 1:42–45

Some things we need to understand, and other things are not
necessary to understand—we need only obey. This story
illustrates that. The cured leper must have been confident
that publicizing Jesus' miraculous cure was a better idea than
obeying Jesus' command to keep silent. I make this mistake
when I act on my own. When I act as part of a group that
decides by consensus what is the best course of action, then
unanticipated consequences are less likely to happen.

Hebrews 3:7–14
Psalm 95:6–7c,8–9,10–11
Mark 1:40–45

What we have heard and know,
and what our fathers have declared to us,
we will declare to the generation to come
the glorious deeds of the LORD and his strength.
—PSALM 78:3–4

I try to tell the young people I know about the amazing things God does in my life. But unfortunately, I often get sidetracked into defending the church's authorities and historical failures. This type of conversation always deflates me and everyone else. When I do manage to keep the topic on God and what God is doing, the response may be incredulity, but at least it is not annoyance. I often give away Miraculous Medals and tell the story of Mary's visit to Catherine Laboure. My mission is to spread the news about what God has done, not to try to defend the church's mishandling of clergy sex abuse against minors.

Hebrews 4:1–5,11
Psalm 78:3 and 4bc,6c–7,8
Mark 2:1–12

The word of God is living and effective,
sharper than a two-edged sword,
penetrating even between soul and spirit,
joints and marrow, and able to discern reflections and thoughts
of the heart.
—HEBREWS 4:12

When our daughter Ellen was teaching English in Japan, some of her adult students asked her questions about the Ten Commandments. They looked skeptical when she told them that coveting someone else's blessings was also a sin. One young woman asked her, "How does your God know?" When Ellen explained that God sees our hearts, the entire room gasped in horror. "He can see your heart? How embarrassing! Can you imagine? Ellen, are you okay with that?" This story makes me laugh, but it also makes me think twice before I let my thoughts ramble into murky places.

Hebrews 4:12–16
Psalm 19:8,9,10,15
Mark 2:13–17

Sunday

JANUARY 17

Then Eli understood that the LORD was calling the youth.
So he said to Samuel,
"Go to sleep, and if you are called, reply,
'Speak, LORD, for your servant is listening.'"
—1 SAMUEL 3:8–9

In the Bible, many people are asleep when God contacts them. Jacob falls asleep before he spends the night wrestling with his holy visitor. His son Joseph hears from God in dreams, as does Joseph, Mary's spouse, generations later. Peter is asleep in prison when God frees him from chains. Old Eli seems to understand this method. He tells Samuel, "Go to sleep, and if you are called, reply. . . ." Perhaps during the day we are too preoccupied to hear God's call. God is forever promising us "rest." The commandment to keep holy the Sabbath day is God's plea for us to lie down and rest so we can hear his call.

1 Samuel 3:3b–10,19
Psalm 40:2,4,7–8,8–9,10(8a,9a)
1 Corinthians 6:13c–15a,17–20
John 1:35–42

JANUARY 18

"Likewise, no one pours new wine into old wineskins.
Otherwise, the wine will burst the skins,
and both the wine and the skins are ruined.
Rather, new wine is poured into fresh wineskins."
—MARK 2:22

Msgr. William Fitzgerald was the parish priest when I was growing up. He had an open door to his rectory, enthusiasm for lay leadership, and abundant love for everyone he met. He supported adult religious education, opened a food pantry, and took the parish on weekend camping trips. Fr. "Fitz" believed fully and enthusiastically that God wants us to stretch. In his eighties, the last sermon I heard him preach was about new wineskins. If Fitz wanted to stretch months before his death, who am I to stay the same? I know that if I want God's new wine, I need to make room inside.

Hebrews 5:1–10
Psalm 110:1,2,3,4
Mark 2:18–22

JANUARY 19

*At this the Pharisees said to him,
"Look, why are they doing what is unlawful
on the sabbath?"*
—MARK 2:23

"Pharisees" are way too interested in sin. They rarely talk
about anything else. When I was volunteering at the
St. Vincent de Paul thrift store, a lady who worked as a
barmaid told me how to tell the difference between churches
where the people believe in God and ones where they don't.
"At first, they all talk about God: God loves you, Jesus loves
you, we love you . . . but after a while some of those places
begin to talk about the devil and sins and evil. Ain't long and
they give up talking about God. They aren't nearly as
interested in God as they are in the devil." I listen carefully in
my church nowadays, and to my own thoughts. Jesus and the
barmaid knew that religion is mostly not about sins.

Hebrew 6:10–20
Psalm 111:1–2,4–5,9 and 10c
Mark 2:23–28

Then he said to the Pharisees,
"Is it lawful to do good on the sabbath rather than
to do evil,
to save life rather than to destroy it?"
But they remained silent.
—MARK 3:4

The Pharisees did not give the obvious answer to Jesus'
question: *Of course it is lawful to do good on the Sabbath.* That
answer would not support their goal of catching Jesus in the
act of violating the picayune Sabbath laws. Here are the
questions that Jesus asks me: Is it lawful to help
undocumented immigrants? Is it lawful to restrict access to
guns? Is it lawful to ban capital punishment and abortion? All
these things go against the laws of our land. The Pharisees, if
they read this, might immediately go out and take counsel
with the Herodians. The Herodians supported Herod, a
person who disgusted the Pharisees because of his adultery.
Adultery didn't offend them as Jesus did.

Hebrews 7:1–3,15–17
Psalm 110:1,2,3,4
Mark 3:1–6

JANUARY 21

• ST. AGNES, VIRGIN AND MARTYR •

*Jesus is always able to save those who approach God
through him,
since he lives forever to make intercession for them.*
—HEBREWS 7:25

Jesus' teachings are full of paradox. "Whoever loses his life
for my sake will save it" (Luke 9:24). "The one who is least
among all of you is the one who is the greatest" (Luke 9:48).
"What man among you having one hundred sheep and losing
one of them would not leave the ninety-nine in the desert
and go after the lost one?" (Luke 15:4). At first glance, this
reading from Hebrews is full of certainty: Jesus is always able
to save those who approach God through him. But he is able
to save us *not because of what we do but because of what he does by
interceding for us.* Yet he asks us to do as much good as we can.
Paradoxy, not certainty, is real religion.

Hebrews 7:25—8:6
Psalm 40:7–8a,8b–9,10,17
Mark 3:7–12

I will be their God,
and they shall be my people.
And they shall not teach, each one his fellow
citizen and kin, saying,
"Know the Lord,"
for all shall know me, from least to greatest.
—HEBREWS 8:10–11

This makes me want to shush my inner teacher. God has sent his Holy Spirit into the world, and I need to believe it. Everyone is a child of God: you, me, the priest, the waitress, the ditch digger, the soldier, the tyrant, the dogcatcher—no exceptions. And we all know God a little bit and can learn from one another.

Hebrews 8:6–13
Psalm 85:8 and 10,11–12,13–14
Mark 3:13–19

God mounts his throne amid shouts of joy;
the LORD, amid trumpet blasts.
Sing praise to God, sing praise;
sing praise to our king, sing praise.
—PSALM 47:6–7

Have you ever wondered why God needs our praise? After all, he is humble, merciful, loving, powerful, and just. What person with those qualities seeks praise from others? No one. It's the proud, the arrogant, and the people uncertain of their power or position who seek praise. Yet not only this psalm but also many others urge us to praise the Lord. If God does not need our praise for his sake, he must need us to praise him for our own sake. So now, the question is, have you ever wondered why we need to praise God?

Hebrews 9:2–3,11–14
Psalm 47:2–3,6–7,8–9
Mark 3:20–21

Jonah began his journey through the city,
and had gone but a single day's walk announcing,
"Forty days more and Nineveh shall be destroyed,"
when the people of Nineveh believed God;
they proclaimed a fast
and all of them, great and small, put on sackcloth.
—JONAH 3:4–5

Jonah was a reluctant prophet. He didn't like the people of Nineveh. He didn't like God's assignment. He didn't like the way God forgave the people when they repented. Yet it appears that Jonah was the only prophet who was successful. He warned the people, and they repented. This story helps me remember that what God asks me to do is not about me; it's about God and all the souls he wants to save. Jonah needed to get over himself, and so do I.

Jonah 3:1–5,10
Psalm 25:4–5,6–7,8–9(4a)
1 Corinthians 7:29–31
Mark 1:14–20

JANUARY 25

• THE CONVERSION OF ST. PAUL THE APOSTLE •

Paul addressed the people in these words:
"I am a Jew, born in Tarsus in Cilicia,
but brought up in this city.
At the feet of Gamaliel I was educated strictly
in our ancestral law and was zealous for God. . . .
Even the high priest and the whole council of elders
can testify on my behalf."
—ACTS 22:3–5

Like Jonah, Saul needed to get over himself. Jesus knocked
him to the ground and temporarily blinded him to get
through to him. I really don't want God to knock me down
to convince me to release my ego. I would much rather read
a nice, safe devotional like this one and come around in my
own good time. I would prefer to be sitting in a church when
God speaks to me, not falling flat on my face in the street. I
like my ego too much.

Acts 22:3–16 or 9:1–22
Psalm 117:1bc,2
Mark 16:15–18

JANUARY 26

• ST. TIMOTHY AND ST. TITUS, BISHOPS •

So do not be ashamed of your testimony to our Lord,
nor of me, a prisoner for his sake;
but bear your share of hardship for the Gospel
with the strength that comes from God.
—2 TIMOTHY 1:8

Sometimes, I don't bear my share of hardship. I whine and criticize and make everyone aware of how displeased I am with the current state of affairs. By doing all these things, I am making other people take on my load. Not fair. And certainly not helpful to anyone. Paul advises Timothy to "bear your share of . . . with the strength that comes from God." Before I open my mouth to complain, I need to ask God for his strength. Mine is so tiny.

2 Timothy 1:1–8 or Titus 1:1–5
Psalm 96:1–2a,2b–3,7–8a,10
Mark 3:31–35

JANUARY 27

• ST. ANGELA MERICI, VIRGIN •

Those present along with the Twelve
questioned him about the parables.
He answered them,
"The mystery of the Kingdom of God
has been granted to you.
But to those outside everything comes
in parables."
—MARK 4:11

It irritates me when someone explains a joke. If it has to be explained, it is no longer funny. It is also tedious when someone belabors a point or insists on their interpretation of a story or an event. These reflections I am writing are only that: reflections. My daughter said to me, "Most of the time when people want reflections, they go to a mirror." That's what I have been doing so far: going to a mirror. I hope you go to a mirror as well when you read the Bible. If I were to explain Jesus' parables, you might miss what he wants you to hear.

Hebrews 10:11–18
Psalm 110:1,2,3,4
Mark 4:1–20

JANUARY 28

• ST. THOMAS AQUINAS, PRIEST AND DOCTOR OF THE CHURCH •

*"The measure with which you measure
will be measured out to you,
and still more will be given to you."*
—MARK 4:24

What spiritual gifts do you have? Ask yourself this question without false humility. If you have a generous heart, admit it. If you are a good listener, don't deny it. Do you persevere hopefully when others give up? Do you forgive easily? Have you the knack of healing wounds or broken hearts? Are you sincere? Do you have faith to the point that God is a real friend to you? Do you love absolutely everyone? Do you think that most people are smarter than you? You are reading these reflections almost every day, so admit that you own a measure of zeal for the Gospels. Now that you have identified your gift, ask for more of it. God wants to give you a good measure.

Hebrews 10:19–25
Psalm 24:1–2,3–4ab,5–6
Mark 4:21–25

JANUARY 29

*You need endurance to do the will of God
and receive what he has promised.*
—HEBREWS 10:36

It sure would be nice if endurance weren't necessary, if
Christianity were easy, and if being good were a matter of a
simple decision. But that's not the way God made the world,
and that's not the way God made us. A new potter needs to
make dozens of mugs before one is good enough to sell. An
apprentice baker doesn't frost a cake beautifully on the first
try. Parents raise their children making mistake after mistake.
We don't decide to quit a bad habit and are never tempted
again. When it comes to goodness and love, endurance is
necessary.

Hebrews 10:32–39
Psalm 37:3–4,5–6,23–24,39–40
Mark 4:26–34

*A violent squall came up and waves were breaking
over the boat,
so that it was already filling up.
Jesus was in the stern, asleep on a cushion.*
—MARK 4:37–38

This story is hilarious. Imagine the apostles, many of them fishermen, putting Jesus in the stern and saying something like, "You go to sleep; we know what we are doing when it comes to sailing. You are a carpenter, not a sailor, so try to stay out of the way." Worldly knowledge gets in the way of my faith, just as it did for the apostles. When I come to the end of my abilities and expertise and everything is filling up with water, only then do I think about waking Jesus and asking his advice. When he sets things right, I have a good chuckle at myself.

Hebrews 11:1–2,8–19
Luke 1:69–70,71–72,73–75
Mark 4:35–41

JANUARY 31

Come, let us sing joyfully to the LORD;
let us acclaim the rock of our salvation.
Let us come into his presence with thanksgiving;
let us joyfully sing psalms to him.
—PSALM 95:1–2

Joy is an essential sign of a Christian. St. Teresa of Ávila wrote, "A sad nun is a bad nun. . . . I am more afraid of one unhappy sister than a crowd of evil spirits. . . . What would happen if we hid what little sense of humor we had? Let each of us humbly use this to cheer others." Notice that she is not implying that we all have the same level of joy. But she is warning us about suppressing "what little sense of humor we had." My father used to say, "Life is basically funny. It has sad parts, but the rest is a good story."

Deuteronomy 18:15–20
Psalm 95:1–2,6–7,7–9(8)
1 Corinthians 7:32–35
Mark 1:21–28

FEBRUARY 1

*(He had been saying to him, "Unclean spirit,
come out of the man!")
He asked him, "What is your name?"
He replied, "Legion is my name. There are many of us."*
—MARK 5:8–9

I believe in the Holy Spirit. I also believe in the unholy
spirits. An example of evil spirits is when a crowd goes
hysterical with fear and rage. When riots, rape, and pillage
occur in a mass attack, that is an evil spirit. There was an evil
spirit running loose in the Rwandan genocide. Evil was on
Calvary. "It can't happen here" is foolishness. It can happen
here because we do not love God and each other enough.
Love, prayer, and humility are the *only* weapons that can
defeat the devil. Jesus showed us that.

Hebrews 11:32–40
Psalm 31:20,21,22,23,24
Mark 5:1–20

FEBRUARY 2

• THE PRESENTATION OF THE LORD •

But who will endure the day of his coming?
And who can stand when he appears?
For he is like the refiner's fire,
or like the fuller's lye.
—MALACHI 3:2

The refiner's fire and the fuller's lye are intended to make gold pure and fabric white. Jesus is coming to make us pure and clean. "Who can stand when he appears?" No one. None of us is pure and clean. I can wait until he appears before I clean up my soul, or I can begin working on it now. There are two certain "day of his coming" events: either at the end of time or at my own personal death. At least one of those will happen in the next forty years. It's already time to begin refining and bleaching.

Malachi 3:1–4
Psalm 24:7,8,9,10
Hebrews 2:14–18
Luke 2:22–40 or 2:22–32

Wednesday

FEBRUARY 3

• ST. BLASE, BISHOP AND MARTYR • ST. ANSGAR, BISHOP •

So he was not able to perform any mighty deed there,
apart from curing a few sick people
by laying his hands on them.
He was amazed at their lack of faith.
—MARK 6:5–6

Jesus was amazed at his townsfolks' lack of faith. Here is my question: Was Jesus amazed that God did not give them faith? Or was Jesus amazed that they were not using the faith given to them? People like me, who are capable of belief, are also capable of being fooled. It can make us cautious. I sympathize with the Nazarenes. Was Jesus the Messiah or not? Was God his father, or did Mary make up the virgin-birth story? Were those Galilean fishermen very clever liars? Had the cured sick people all faked their ailments? Maybe his friends and relatives had faith but they were afraid to use it.

Hebrews 12:4–7,11–15
Psalm 103:1–2,13–14,17–18a
Mark 6:1–6

*Jesus summoned the Twelve and
began to send them out two by two
and gave them authority over unclean spirits.*
—MARK 6:7

As members of the Society of St. Vincent de Paul, we are instructed to always go out two by two. We visit people in their homes, just as the apostles did. Every so often, one of our members says, "Can I just go by myself? No one else is free, and I'm sure it will be a quick visit." The answer is no. Apart from safety and liability reasons, apart from ensuring the protection of vulnerable people, and apart from not flouting agreed-upon procedure, going alone shows an unwise belief in ourselves. Jesus sent out the twelve two by two. They did not send themselves; they were sent, and they were told to stick together. As Vincentians, we are sent exactly the same way.

Hebrews 12:18–19,21–24
Psalm 48:2–3ab,3cd–4,9,10–11
Mark 6:7–13

The LORD is my light and my salvation;
whom should I fear?
—PSALM 27:1

He promptly dispatched an executioner
with orders to bring back his head.
He went off and beheaded him in the prison.
—MARK 6:27

Here are two Scripture verses, one from Psalm 27 telling us not to be afraid of anyone, and one from Mark about Herod ordering the beheading of John the Baptist. It's confusing that these two readings are on the same day. What are we to make of this contradiction? The only conclusion I come to is that if I, or anyone else, quotes the Bible and claims to know exactly what God is saying, we are fools. The Bible is complicated.

Hebrews 13:1–8
Psalm 27:1,3,5,8b–9abc
Mark 6:14–29

FEBRUARY 6

• ST. PAUL MIKI AND COMPANIONS, MARTYRS •

His heart was moved with pity for them,
for they were like sheep without a shepherd.
—MARK 6:34

I saw a demonstration of Border Collies herding sheep. The shepherd stood by himself, apart from the flock, made hand signals to the two dogs, called out simple orders, and whistled. I was impressed by the skills of the dogs until the sheep got spooked. Suddenly, the lead sheep ran in amongst us spectators, and all the others followed. The dogs were frantic to separate the flock from the humans, but it got messy. People snatched up their children and shrieked. The shepherd stopped calling to the dogs and instead called out to the whirling people, "Just hold your places. Stand still and the dogs will sort it out." Once we all stood still, that is what happened. We needed the shepherd more than the sheep needed him.

Hebrews 13:15–17,20–21
Psalm 23:1–3a,3b–4,5,6
Mark 6:30–34

Sunday

FEBRUARY 7

• FIFTH SUNDAY IN ORDINARY TIME •

If in bed I say, "When shall I arise?"
then the night drags on;
I am filled with restlessness until the dawn.
—JOB 7:4

I listened to a podcast about a scientist who attempted to
verify whether, as often claimed, people solve problems
while they are asleep. He had the participants play the
computer game Tetris before going to bed. If he woke them
in the middle of the night and asked what they were
dreaming, they were often going in circles playing the game.
If he woke them close to dawn, they were usually
categorizing the problems and organizing possible solutions.
Job had every problem possible. His brain was whirling all
night long. Jesus, in the Gospel, rose before dawn and "went
off to a deserted place, where he prayed." So, this is what I
think: If my problems are going to ruin my sleep, why not
get up and pray?

Job 7:1–4,6–7
Psalm 147:1–2,3–4,5–6
1 Corinthians 9:16–19,22–23
Mark 1:29–39

FEBRUARY 8

*In the beginning, when God created the heavens
and the earth,
the earth was a formless wasteland,
and darkness covered the abyss,
while a mighty wind swept over the waters.*
—GENESIS 1:1–2

This is how everything began: formless, dark, moving wherever the wind blew it. God had an idea that it could be more interesting, more purposeful, and more varied. We are part of God's idea as well. In our mothers' wombs we began formless, dark, and helpless. Physicists tell us that the universe is expanding, always expanding. God's ideas are going out in all directions. God is not out of ideas. God will never run out of ideas.

Genesis 1:1–19
Psalm 104:1–2a,5–6,10 and 12,24 and 35c
Mark 6:53–56

FEBRUARY 9

*God created man in his image;
in the divine image he created him;
male and female he created them.*
—GENESIS 1:27

Dorothy Sayers, in *The Mind of the Maker*, points out that the Bible tells us God made us in his image, but at this point in the narrative, the only thing we know about God is that he creates. God hasn't done anything except make things. So, if we are made in God's image, it follows that we are creators. I try not to neglect this essential part of who I am. I bake cookies, paint, write, plant gardens, sing, and bring people together. It is not in my nature to spend all my time cleaning, repairing, maintaining, sorting, and storing. God made me like him. I am created to make things happen, not keep things the same.

Genesis 1:20—2:4a
Psalm 8:4–5,6–7,8–9
Mark 7:1–13

FEBRUARY 10

• ST. SCHOLASTICA, VIRGIN •

Out of the ground the Lord God
made various trees grow
that were delightful to look at and good for food,
with the tree of life in the middle of the garden
and the tree of the knowledge of good and evil.
—GENESIS 2:9

We live on an acre of ground with many mature trees around the property. When our daughters were young, I once gave them the job of counting how many trees grew in our yard. They thought this was great fun. They counted more than eighty trees! I was surprised by the number.

The last few years have been hard on the trees. We have had to take down dozens that have succumbed to the shifting climate. It makes me sad to see holes in the canopy. God did not create people to represent life or the knowledge of good and evil. He made trees for these purposes. We need trees.

Genesis 2:4b–9,15–17
Psalm 104:1–2a,27–28,29bc–30
Mark 7:14–23

FEBRUARY 11

Jesus went to the district of Tyre.
He entered a house and wanted no one to know about it,
but he could not escape notice.
—MARK 7:24

Jesus has traveled far from his normal territory. He tries to take a break and escape a lot of attention, but people find out soon enough where he is staying. This will happen if he resides in us, as well. People will notice that something has changed, that Jesus is present.

Genesis 2:18–25
Psalm 128:1–2,3,4–5
Mark 7:24–30

Now the serpent was the most cunning of all the animals
that the LORD God had made.
—GENESIS 3:1

God makes Paradise: a beautiful garden for Adam and Eve to live in. And then . . . he puts a cunning snake in there with them. What's up with that? Just when you think everything is going perfectly—*bam!* Even paradise had its problems. I guess this is why God is described so often as "a shield," or "a savior," or "a shelter from the storm," or "a healer." We will always need God.

Genesis 3:1–8
Psalm 32:1–2,5,6,7
Mark 7:31–37

Then the LORD God said: "See!
The man has become like one of us,
knowing what is good and what is evil!
Therefore, he must not be allowed to put out his hand
to take fruit from the tree of life also,
and thus eat of it and live forever."
—GENESIS 3:22

This story seems to be saying that people have power that God doesn't give them. Of course, we know that we can always say no to God. We have the power to do evil, to sin, to be selfish. God doesn't want us acting this way, but we have that power. It makes me think that perhaps, if I stay close to God like Adam and Eve were in the garden, I also receive power just from that closeness. Not only the power to live forever, but the power to heal, to love enemies, to forgive, to spread joy.

Genesis 3:9–24
Psalm 90:2,3–4abc,5–6,12–13
Mark 8:1–10

Then I acknowledged my sin to you,
my guilt I covered not.
I said, "I confess my faults to the LORD,"
and you took away the guilt of my sin.
—PSALM 32:5

Explanations are akin to casting blame or making an excuse for our misbehavior. According to Psalm 32, God doesn't need an explanation or an excuse, only an apology. He is waiting to forgive us.

Leviticus 13:1–2,44–46
Psalm 32:1–2,5,11,(7)
1 Corinthians 10:31—11:1
Mark 1:40–45

FEBRUARY 15

> So the LORD said to Cain,
> "Why are you so resentful and crestfallen?
> If you do well, you can hold up your head;
> but if not, sin is a demon lurking at the door:
> his urge is toward you, yet you can be his master."
> —GENESIS 4:6–7

God always speaks the truth. He would not tell us that we can be the master of our own sin if we were incapable of it. St. Vincent de Paul wrote this: "The most powerful weapon to conquer the devil is humility. For, as he does not know at all how to employ it, neither does he know how to defend himself from it." Apparently, all Cain needed to conquer the devil was humility. That's all I need as well. I don't always want it—that's a problem.

Genesis 4:1–15,25
Psalm 50:1,8,16bc–17,20–21
Mark 8:11–13

FEBRUARY 16

When the LORD saw how great was man's wickedness
on earth, and how no desire that his heart conceived
was ever anything but evil,
he regretted that he had made man on the earth,
and his heart was grieved.
—GENESIS 6:5–6

Why did God allow evil on the earth? If he is a loving God, why all the suffering and pain? Every believer either asks this question or is asked it. My atheist friend taps the table and says to me, "If God exists, and God is good, then explain children with cancer to me." I can't, of course. My religion does not explain floods, lightning strikes, volcanoes, or childhood cancer. My religion says that God's "heart was grieved" over humanity's wickedness, and God put a temporary halt to it, and will someday wipe it out permanently. God allows the floods and the cancer. Those do not grieve his heart like wickedness.

Genesis 6:5–8; 7:1–5,10
Psalm 29:1a and 2,3ac–4,3b and 9c–10
Mark 8:14–21

FEBRUARY 17

• ASH WEDNESDAY •

Jesus said to his disciples:
"Take care not to perform righteous deeds
in order that people may see them."
—MATTHEW 6:1

Does anyone else ever squirm in church on Ash Wednesday?
The Gospel admonishes us not to pray in public, not to give
alms in front of everyone, and to wash our faces when we are
fasting. Then we go to church (sometimes having to take
time off work so our coworkers know where we are!), put
money in a basket that is passed around, and wear ashes on
our foreheads all day long. It feels like the people who stay
home praying, fasting, and sending a donation in the mail are
following Jesus' teaching much better than I am doing it by
going to church. I start off Lent feeling hypocritical and
sinful on the very first day! Wait. Maybe that's the
whole idea?

Joel 2:12–18
Psalm 51:3–4,5–6ab,12–13,14 and 17
2 Corinthians 5:20—6:2
Matthew 6:1–6,16–18

Jesus said to his disciples:
"The Son of Man must suffer greatly and be rejected
by the elders, the chief priests, and the scribes,
and be killed and on the third day be raised."

Then he said to all,
"If anyone wishes to come after me,
he must deny himself
and take up his cross daily and follow me."
—LUKE 9:22–23

Think on this: If we wish to follow Jesus into great suffering, rejection, grizzly execution, and finally resurrection, then we need to stop complaining and do the things he did, namely: healing, preaching, loving our enemies, and lots of praying. To be honest, the only parts that appeal to me about this program are resurrection, healing, and prayer. I have a long way to go.

Deuteronomy 30:15–20
Psalm 1:1–2,3,4 and 6
Luke 9:22–25

For you are not pleased with sacrifices;
should I offer a burnt offering, you would not accept it.
My sacrifice, O God, is a contrite spirit;
a heart contrite and humbled, O God, you will not spurn.
—PSALM 51:18–19

Seldom do I remember being truly contrite. The two times I was pulled over for traffic violations—which I clearly committed—I was not contrite. My mind was whirling with all kinds of excuses, mostly based on ignorance of the speed limit. I do not remember apologizing to the officer. I was simply not contrite. Another time, I mistakenly gave my young daughter twice the amount of medicine, then called Poison Control in a panic, and was shaken and relieved to learn that it wasn't a harmful overdose. Again, I blurted out excuses, not apologies. Clearly, contriteness does not come easily.

Isaiah 58:1–9a
Psalm 51:3–4,5–6ab,18–19
Matthew 9:14–15

Jesus said to them in reply,
"Those who are healthy do not need a physician,
but the sick do.
I have not come to call the righteous
to repentance but sinners."
—LUKE 5:31–32

This situation reminds me of high school. A whole bunch of students get their work done and are ready for the test, but several others moan about the difficulty of the subject matter and ask the teacher for another day to study. The teacher doesn't want them to flunk the test, so he postpones it and goes over the material again. Those who were ready now moan that they have other tests to study for and don't want them piled up together. The teacher isn't going to rescind his mercy for the first group. Those who were ready will have to deal with the delay and not be resentful toward their classmates or the teacher.

Isaiah 58:9b–14
Psalm 86:1–2,3–4,5–6
Luke 5:27–32

FEBRUARY 21

• FIRST SUNDAY OF LENT •

The Spirit drove Jesus out into the desert,
and he remained in the desert for forty days,
tempted by Satan.
—MARK 1:12–13

Have you ever felt as if God put you into a waiting room and then forgot you? Maybe you tried to sit still, pray, read some magazines, discern your next move, and rest. But after a while, it felt as if the office staff called all the other people waiting in the room, took care of them, and then went out for lunch. The forty days in the desert must have seemed like that to Jesus. He was baptized and ready for action; then "the Spirit" sent him off to the desert. And he waited. He prayed, he fasted, and he still waited. So he prayed some more, continued to fast, and began to be tempted to make his own bread, demand God's attention, and take control. Instead, he waited.

Genesis 9:8–15
Psalm 25:4–5,6–7,8–9
1 Peter 3:18–22
Mark 1:12–15

FEBRUARY 22

Do not lord it over those assigned to you,
but be examples to the flock.
—1 PETER 5:3

Leadership is always difficult; especially leadership that is assigned, not democratically elected. I wonder how Peter felt when Jesus told him he was going to be the "rock" on which the church would be built? By the time First Peter was written, the church had many presbyters, and all the leadership issues of a growing organization must have been on Peter's plate. His advice to the middle managers? "Do not lord it over" and "be examples to the flock." Surely, this was the way Jesus led, and Peter as well. For an unelected official, it is the only workable way to manage people.

1 Peter 5:1–4
Psalm 23:1–3a,4,5,6
Matthew 16:13–19

FEBRUARY 23

• ST. POLYCARP, BISHOP AND MARTYR •

I sought the LORD, and he answered me
and delivered me from all my fears.
—PSALM 34:5

Psalm 34 does not say that the Lord delivers us from all dangers, temptations, or evildoers. The Lord delivers us from our own fears. We are afraid of danger, temptation, and evil people—that is our flaw. We don't pray rightly; rather, we pray for the world as it exists to be different. We ought to pray that *we* are different, not the world. We need to pray for fearlessness no matter what the world throws at us.

Isaiah 55:10–11
Psalm 34:4–5,6–7,16–17,18–19
Matthew 6:7–15

*"Man and beast shall be covered with sackcloth and
call loudly to God;
every man shall turn from his evil way
and from the violence he has in hand.
Who knows, God may relent and forgive,
and withhold his blazing wrath,
so that we shall not perish."*
—JONAH 3:8–9

The book of Jonah, like much of the Bible, tells us about how important it is to repent and to turn from our ways back to God's ways. How seldom I actually do this! I like my ways. I like to think that I am wise and good and that other people need to be better, not me. I think, "If everyone would only listen to God, then the world would be saved." I seldom think, "If I would change the way I live, ask God's forgiveness, and forgive others, then God would forgive me 'so that we shall not perish.'"

Jonah 3:1–10
Psalm 51:3–4,12–13,18–19
Luke 11:29–32

FEBRUARY 25

"Now help me, who am alone and have no one but you,
O LORD, my God."
—ESTHER C:25

The story of Queen Esther is of someone living in a place of
luxury, sticking her neck out to save people in peril. It is also
a story of irrevocable decrees and bloody vengeance.
Irrevocable laws leave the lawmakers in the position of not
being able to adjust to changing circumstances. Bloody
vengeance creates tit for tat and endless years of retaliation.
Esther calls on God for deliverance. God answers. But
because the original decree calling for the destruction of the
Jews is irrevocable, Esther requests revenge against their
enemies who can still lawfully kill them. Jesus, in contrast,
says, "Do to others whatever you would have them do to
you." No irrevocable laws here, only mercy.

Esther C:12,14–16,23–25
Psalm 138:1–2ab,2cde–3,7c–8
Matthew 7:7–12

And if the virtuous man turns from the path
of virtue to do evil,
the same kind of abominable things that the
wicked man does,
can he do this and still live?
None of his virtuous deeds shall be remembered,
because he has broken faith and committed sin;
because of this, he shall die.
—EZEKIEL 18:24

The ends do not justify the means. My previous virtues do not justify my committing evil in the name of good. This is entirely clear in this passage from Ezekiel. It is entirely clear in the life of Jesus Christ as well. He is without sin. He commits no evil, even upon his enemies who kill him in the name of God.

Ezekiel 18:21–28
Psalm 130:1–2,3–4,5–7a,7bc–8
Matthew 5:20–26

FEBRUARY 27

"But I say to you, love your enemies,
and pray for those who persecute you,
that you may be children of your heavenly Father,
for he makes his sun rise on the bad and the good,
and causes rain to fall on the just and the unjust."
—MATTHEW 5:44–45

Sunshine and rain are essential for life and growth, and God provides both of these to everyone, no matter if we are good or evil. He asks us, his children, to do the same. What sunshine or rain do I withhold? The sunshine of a smile to cocky teens? The rain of coins to street people with their hands out? The sunshine of raising my voice in song during Mass? The rain of a generous tip to the bumbling waiter? I have no right to withhold love from anyone.

Deuteronomy 26:16–19
Psalm 119:1–2,4–5,7–8
Matthew 5:43–48

FEBRUARY 28

• SECOND SUNDAY OF LENT •

Then a cloud came, casting a shadow over them;
from the cloud came a voice,
"This is my beloved Son. Listen to him."
—MARK 9:7

Picture the scene: *Jesus and his apostles have climbed a small mountain, a vision of dead prophets appears, and a voice comes from the clouds.* If I had been there, what would I expect the voice to say? A voice from the clouds should have a big announcement, something I don't know already. But no, this voice says that Jesus is God's son—already knew that—and that he is worth listening to—knew that as well. I am always searching the Scriptures or theology or testimonials for something new. I want fresh information, but God keeps repeating himself. Could he think, perhaps, that I am not listening?

Genesis 22:1–2,9a,10–13,15–18
Psalm 116:10,15,16–17,18–19
Romans 8:31b–34
Mark 9:2–10

O LORD, we are shame-faced like our kings,
our princes, and our fathers,
for having sinned against you.
But yours, O Lord, our God, are compassion
and forgiveness!
—DANIEL 9:8–9

The Old Testament is full of verses like this one. The people
have sinned and admit it, begging for God's merciful
forgiveness. The New Testament records the bumbling
nonunderstanding of the apostles and their desertion of
Jesus. Paul's letters scold the new Christians for being selfish
and lazy. Why would today's Christians ever boast about
ourselves or our works? We are spiritual descendants of
sinners, cowards, and slack-offs, and it shows. We do have a
fantastic God, however. God is all that we have that's worth
talking about. There is joy in that only.

Daniel 9:4b–10
Psalm 79:8,9,11 and 13
Luke 6:36–38

MARCH 2

Come now, let us set things right,
says the LORD:
Though your sins be like scarlet,
they may become white as snow;
Though they be crimson red,
they may become white as wool.
—ISAIAH 1:18

Come now, let us set things right, says the LORD. This sounds exactly like my dad. If I was stacking alphabet blocks and they all collapsed, he would lean over and help me set them up again. If I was struggling to figure out algebra, nearly in tears with frustration, he would look at my notebook and suggest a possible step. If my car wouldn't start, he would open the hood and check the battery. God is a good father. He wants to help us set things right. We only need to ask.

Isaiah 1:10,16–20
Psalm 50:8–9,16bc–17,21 and 23
Matthew 23:1–12

Wednesday

MARCH 3

• ST. KATHARINE DREXEL, VIRGIN •

*Whoever wishes to be great among you shall
be your servant;
whoever wishes to be first among you
shall be your slave.*
—MATTHEW 20:26–27

St. Katharine Drexel was born rich and high up in society.
When her father died, his estate was worth $1.5
million—$400 million in today's dollars. It was divided
amongst charities and his three daughters. Katharine used
her portion of this fortune to build schools for African
American and Native American children and to support poor
people in many ways. St. Katharine was born great by the
measure of our society. It was her dream to become great in
God's eyes by becoming the servant of the poor. She was a
serious Jesus fan.

Jeremiah 18:18–20
Psalm 31:5–6,14,15–16
Matthew 20:17–28

Thursday

MARCH 4

I, the LORD, alone probe the mind
and test the heart,
To reward everyone according to his ways,
according to the merit of his deeds.
—JEREMIAH 17:10

People under pressure sometimes act in ways that go against their own best selves and contrary to their highest convictions. God alone can read their hearts. God alone understands the intentions even when the deeds appear wrong to us. We see only their actions; we cannot see hearts. A wise member of the Society of St. Vincent de Paul once told me that there are three rules to follow for being a Vincentian: do not judge, and do not judge, and do not judge.

Jeremiah 17:5–10
Psalm 1:1–2,3,4 and 6
Luke 16:19–31

> *When the chief priests and the Pharisees heard*
> *his parables,*
> *they knew that he was speaking about them.*
> —MATTHEW 21:45

Just like the chief priests and the Pharisees, when I am guilty, I know I am guilty, and I don't like it when someone points out my wrongdoing. It is said that, on average, a person runs one hundred red lights before he or she is pulled over for the infraction. When the officer walks up to our car window, I'm willing to bet that very few of us confess to the previous ninety-nine. It's probably like that for most of our sins.

Genesis 37:3–4,12–13a,17b–28a
Psalm 105:16–17,18–19,20–21
Matthew 21:33–43,45–46

*Tax collectors and sinners were all drawing near
to listen to Jesus,
but the Pharisees and scribes began
to complain, saying,
"This man welcomes sinners and eats with them."*
—LUKE 15:1–2

The bad guys in the Gospels are not the criminals, the extortionists, the prostitutes, and the people who ignore the Sabbath-day regulations. The bad guys, the ones who end up plotting to kill Jesus, are the religious leaders. They are the ones who read the Scriptures, quote the prophets, donate money to the coffers, and follow the precepts exactly. They also don't like to share meals with sinners. That describes me, as well. I am in grave danger of losing my soul.

Micah 7:14–15,18–20
Psalm 103:1–2,3–4,9–10,11–12
Luke 15:1–3,11–32

In those days, God delivered all these commandments:
"I, the LORD, am your God,
who brought you out of the land of Egypt,
that place of slavery.
You shall not have other gods besides me."
—EXODUS 20:1–3

When do I have other gods? Perhaps when I love something
more than I love God? The problem is that I'm not entirely
sure that I love God. I know I love my husband and my
daughters. I would gladly give up everything I own for them.
In addition, I would give up my life, my health, my
reputation, and my work. I really, really love them. I'm not
yet there with God. Not yet, not yet. God is so patient.

Exodus 20:1–17 or 20:1–3,7–8,12–17
Psalm 19:8,9,10,11
1 Corinthians 1:22–25
John 2:13–25

But his servants came up and reasoned with him.
"My father," they said,
"if the prophet had told you to do something
extraordinary,
would you not have done it?
All the more now, since he said to you,
and be clean, should you do as he said."
So Naaman went down and plunged
into the Jordan seven times
at the word of the man of God.
His flesh became again like the flesh
of a little child, and he was clean.
—2 KINGS 5:13–14

Does God ask us to do extraordinary things? He asks us to
obey the Ten Commandments, be humble, pray, confess our
wrongdoing, forgive, take care of the poor, and believe in
him. Love God and love our neighbor, and we will
become clean.

2 Kings 5:1–15b
Psalm 42:2,3; 43:3,4
Luke 4:24–30

Peter approached Jesus and asked him,
"Lord, if my brother sins against me,
how often must I forgive him?
As many as seven times?"
Jesus answered, "I say to you, not seven times
but seventy-seven times."
—MATTHEW 18:21–22

Forgiving children multiple times is not difficult. Forgiving unintentional harm is possible given time to heal the wounds. But someone who repeatedly and intentionally harms another—that is abuse. I don't think Jesus wants us to put ourselves or others in dangerous situations because of our determination to forgive. He wouldn't be a very good person, let alone a good God, if he required that. It's good to walk away from abuse. Jesus left town many times when people threatened or verbally abused him. Forgiveness can come later, after safety is secured. We do not have to be someone's punching bag.

Daniel 3:25,34–43
Psalm 25:4–5ab,6 and 7bc,8 and 9
Matthew 18:21–35

*"However, take care and be earnestly on your guard
not to forget the things which your own eyes
have seen,
nor let them slip from your memory as long
as you live,
but teach them to your children and to your
children's children."*
—DEUTERONOMY 5:9

Remembering what my own eyes have seen is a practice in gratefulness. My own eyes have seen good people beyond counting and blessings without number. My eyes have seen the birth of my children and the passing of my parents. I have seen terrible accidents but many, many more near misses. My eyes have seen angry people, but laughter and smiles have outpaced them. My eyes have seen want, and they have seen the providence of God. I have seen saints. These are the things I teach my children.

Deuteronomy 4:1,5–9
Psalm 147:12–13,15–16,19–20
Matthew 5:17–19

Thus says the LORD:
This is what I commanded my people:
Listen to my voice;
then I will be your God and you shall be
my people.
—JEREMIAH 7:23

How, exactly, are we to listen to the voice of God? One way is through contemplation. In the fourteenth-century classic *The Cloud of Unknowing*, written by an anonymous English mystic, the author writes, "This is what you are to do: lift your heart up to the Lord with a gentle stirring of love, desiring him for his own sake and not for his gifts. Center all your attention and desire on him. . . . Do all in your power to forget everything else." Contemplation is a lot like listening to our best friend—which is what God wants to be for us.

Jeremiah 7:23–28
Psalm 95:1–2,6–7,8–9
Luke 11:14–23

Friday

MARCH 12

One of the scribes came to Jesus and asked him,
"Which is the first of all the commandments?"
Jesus replied, "The first is this:
Hear, O Israel!
The Lord our God is Lord alone!
You shall love the Lord your God with all your heart,
with all your soul,
with all your mind,
and with all your strength.
The second is this:
You shall love your neighbor as yourself.
There is no other commandment greater than these."
—MARK 12:28–31

After Jesus gave this answer, the scribe repeated it back to
him. Then Jesus told the man that he was "not far from the
Kingdom of God." Today, like the scribe, try repeating Jesus'
answer to yourself, several times, whenever you can. Do it
again tomorrow. And the next day. This answer is the essence
of what we are seeking.

Hosea 14:2–10
Psalm 81:6c–8a,8bc–9,10–11ab,14 and 17
Mark 12:28–34

MARCH 13

For you are not pleased with sacrifices;
should I offer a burnt offering, you would not accept it.
My sacrifice, O God, is a contrite spirit;
a heart contrite and humbled, O God, you will not spurn.
—PSALM 51:18–19

Once, a priest gave me Psalm 51 to read as my penance after confession. I read it over a few times and meditated on possible reasons why Father had asked me to pray with it. My conclusion was that I probably didn't appear contrite during my confession. I admit that sometimes I mention my sins but do not feel like beating my breast over them. A truly contrite spirit is not easy. Fasting, almsgiving, and burnt offerings are all easier.

Hosea 6:1–6
Psalm 51:3–4,18–19,20–21ab
Luke 18:9–14

*"For everyone who does wicked things hates the light
and does not come toward the light,
so that his works may not be exposed.
But whoever lives the truth comes to the light,
so that his works may be clearly seen as done in God."*
—JOHN 3:20–21

In this passage Jesus is talking to Nicodemus, *who came to him
at night.* Nicodemus is a conflicted member of the Sanhedrin
who is sneaking around to talk with Jesus without anyone
knowing about it. He is doing a good thing by seeking Jesus,
but he is still afraid of the light of day and criticism from his
peers. Keeping societal norms can give us good structures for
our lives, but they can also keep us from being the best we
can be.

2 Chronicles 36:14–16,19–23
Psalm 137:1–2,3,4–5,6(6ab)
Ephesians 2:4–10
John 3:14–21

For his anger lasts but a moment;
a lifetime, his good will.
At nightfall, weeping enters in,
but with the dawn, rejoicing.
—PSALM 30:6

Last night I woke up worrying about the problems of the people in my life. This kept me tossing and turning until I prayed and gradually resumed sleeping, only to wake again and again. In the morning, when Dean and I were saying our prayers together, I said, "God help the billion people in the world who are under pressure." Dean paused, then said, "7.5 billion, Lord." I laughed. True. Why leave anyone out? *With the dawn, rejoicing.*

Isaiah 65:17–21
Psalm 30:2 and 4,5–6,11–12a and 13b
John 4:43–54

Tuesday

MARCH 16

One man was there who had been ill
for thirty-eight years.
When Jesus saw him lying there
and knew that he had been ill for a long time,
he said to him,
"Do you want to be well?"
—JOHN 5:5–6

"Do you want to be well?" Such a strange question. If a doctor said this to me, I would hurl the blood-pressure cuff at her. Not this man. He explains to Jesus that he doesn't have anyone to help him get better. Jesus doesn't argue with that excuse. He cures the man and tells him to get up and carry his own mat. The Gospel does not record that the man was particularly grateful. Later, Jesus tells him to not sin anymore, to which his response is to inform Jesus' enemies. I kind of wonder if that guy wanted to be well? Maybe he didn't like carrying his own mat.

Ezekiel 47:1–9,12
Psalm 46:2–3,5–6,8–9
John 5:1–16

Wednesday

MARCH 17

Jesus answered and said to them,
"Amen, amen, I say to you, the Son cannot
do anything on his own,
but only what he sees the Father doing;
for what he does, the Son will do also. . . .
Nor does the Father judge anyone,
but he has given all judgment to the Son."
—JOHN 5:19,22

Jesus is so completely connected to the Father that he doesn't view his actions as separate from the Father's actions. And we are called to follow Jesus. We are called to not do anything on our own but what we see God doing. And what is God doing? He is creating. He is forgiving. He is waiting patiently. He is calling us. He is healing, teaching, pruning, and loving us. He gave the judging job to Jesus probably because Jesus knows what our lives are like from firsthand experience. Jesus doesn't need our help with judging.

Isaiah 49:8–15
Psalm 145:8–9,13cd–14,17–18
John 5:17–30

Thursday

MARCH 18

• ST. CYRIL OF JERUSALEM, BISHOP AND DOCTOR OF THE CHURCH •

"You search the Scriptures,
because you think you have eternal life through them;
even they testify on my behalf.
But you do not want to come to me to have life."
—JOHN 5:39–40

So, here you and I are searching the Scriptures, trying to save ourselves through them. But Jesus is pleading, "You do not want to come to me to have life." For years, I hoped that I could be saved by reading about God, listening to sermons, attending Mass, saying prayers, dedicating my life to good works, and understanding God. Nope. It doesn't work that way. Those are all good actions, but God wants our hearts, not our works. He wants us to sit still and listen. But keeping busy is easier than listening. That's why the Israelites made a golden calf.

Exodus 32:7–14
Psalm 106:19–20,21–22,23
John 5:31–47

The angel of the Lord appeared to him in a dream
and said,
"Joseph, son of David,
do not be afraid to take Mary your wife
into your home.
For it is through the Holy Spirit
that this child has been conceived in her."
—MATTHEW 1:20

Do not be afraid to take Mary into your home. Place her statue on your dresser. Hang her picture in your living room. Wear her medal around your neck. Do not be afraid; do not be afraid, "for it is through the Holy Spirit that this child has been conceived in her." Joseph was the first to honor Mary. He was the first to take her into his home. I love St. Joseph!

2 Samuel 7:4–5a,12–14a,16
Psalm 89:2–3,4–5,27 and 29
Romans 4:13,16–18,22
Matthew 1:16,18–21,24a or Luke 2:41–51a

The guards answered, "Never before has anyone spoken like this one." So the Pharisees answered them, "Have you also been deceived? Have any of the authorities or the Pharisees believed in him? But this crowd, which does not know the law, is accursed." Nicodemus, one of their members who had come to him earlier, said to them, "Does our law condemn a man before it first hears him and finds out what he is doing?" They answered and said to him, "You are not from Galilee also, are you? Look and see that no prophet arises from Galilee."

—JOHN 7:46–52

Jesus' enemies insult their own guards. They misuse lawful authority and claim that everyone of importance is on their side. When one of their own defends the law, they use prejudice to condemn him and an entire region. Mercy, Lord; we do these things today.

Jeremiah 11:18–20
Psalm 7:2–3,9bc–10,11–12
John 7:40–53

In the days when Christ Jesus was in the flesh,
he offered prayers and supplications
with loud cries and tears
to the one who was able to save him from death,
and he was heard because of his reverence.
—HEBREWS 5:7

Jesus prayed with "loud cries and tears." Prayer is essential to save us from death. Not from dying—we will all go through the tunnel of dying. But we will be saved from eternal death and given eternal life through prayer. What is prayer? It is a tiny spark of faith. Prayer is the humility to beg for help. It is the joy that says, "I have a friend who hears me!" Prayer is the place to rest our weary heads. Prayer is peace that all will be okay in the end. Try prayer. Trust in prayer.

Jeremiah 31:31–34
Psalm 51:3–4,12–13,14–15(12a)
Hebrews 5:7–9
John 12:20–33

*"Let the one among you who is without sin
be the first to throw a stone at her."*
—JOHN 8:7

They dragged the woman who had been caught in the act of
adultery before Jesus. They did not drag the man who had
been caught. I guess they only wanted to stone the woman.
Jesus did not point out this injustice. He knew they were out
to get him as much as to get her. They wanted to force him
either to be merciless or to break the law of Moses. Instead,
he forced them to admit their own sinfulness. He is always
merciful. It is we who condemn ourselves.

Daniel 13:1–9,15–17,19–30,33–62 or 13:41c–62
Psalm 23:1–3a,3b–4,5,6
John 8:1–11

Tuesday

MARCH 23

• ST. TORIBIO DE MOGROVEJO, BISHOP •

"The LORD looked down from his holy height,
from heaven he beheld the earth,
To hear the groaning of the prisoners,
to release those doomed to die."
—PSALM 102:20–21

Psalm 102 says the Lord "looked down from his holy height."
The reading from Numbers describes Moses lifting a bronze
serpent on a pole and telling the Israelites to look up at it and
live. In John's Gospel, Jesus predicts that he, too, will be
lifted up. Many times, leaders preface prayers with "Bow your
heads and pray." I obey them, but it feels unnatural. When I
pray, I look up. It is not that I lack reverence or respect,
because I often pray on my knees. When I am listening, I
close my eyes, but my head remains erect. When I laugh,
sing, or greet people, I look up. When I cry, I look down.
Perhaps God was crying?

Numbers 21:4–9
Psalm 102:2–3,16–18,19–21
John 8:21–30

*King Nebuchadnezzar's face became livid with utter rage
against Shadrach, Meshach, and Abednego.
He ordered the furnace to be heated seven times
more than usual
and had some of the strongest men in his army
bind Shadrach, Meshach, and Abednego
and cast them into the white-hot furnace.*
—DANIEL 3:19–20

This is a pretty good description of the rage I feel when I
can't get people to do what I tell them to do. Lucky for the
world that I am not a king. God knew better than to give me
the gift of power. I deeply respect people who hold power
yet control their tempers.

Daniel 3:14–20,91–92,95
Daniel 3:52,53,54,55,56
John 8:31–42

Thursday

MARCH 25

• THE ANNUNCIATION OF THE LORD •

Therefore the Lord himself will give you this sign:
the virgin shall be with child, and bear a son,
and shall name him Emmanuel,
which means "God is with us!"
—ISAIAH 7:14, 8:10

"God is with us." "I will never leave you." "You are not orphans." "The Kingdom of God is within you." "The souls of the just are in the hands of God." "Do you not know that you are the temple of God and that the Spirit of God dwells in you?" "The Lord is near to all who call upon him." "Behold, I am with you always, until the end of the age."

When will I decide to believe this—really believe this?

Isaiah 7:10–14; 8:10
Psalm 40:7–8a,8b–9,10,11
Hebrews 10:4–10
Luke 1:26–38

In my distress I called upon the LORD
and cried out to my God;
From his temple he heard my voice,
and my cry to him reached his ears.
—PSALM 18:7

I pray every day, and sometimes this psalm is very real: "my cry to him reached his ears." What do I mean by this? Here is an example: Yesterday I prayed for an increase in peace for my immediate family. Today, we were all sending Snapchats back and forth full of jokes, funny photos, and pink hearts. I did not begin the string of messages, but I jumped into it with joy. Thank you, God, for hearing my cry! So, today, I prayed for peace in the Church. I probably won't get a Snapchat from the hierarchy, but I know my cry reached God's ears.

Jeremiah 20:10–13
Psalm 18:2–3a,3bc–4,5–6,7
John 10:31–42

So from that day on they planned to kill him.

So Jesus no longer walked about in public
among the Jews,
but he left for the region near the desert,
to a town called Ephraim,
and there he remained with his disciples.
—JOHN 11:53–54

Jesus began his ministry by going to the desert, and before
his passion, he went back to a town near the desert. There
are crucial times in my life when I find myself sitting still. A
decision or change needs to be made, or has been made for
me, so I need to regroup and think and pray. The first few
times this happened, I fought against the upheaval and
inactivity. Now when life takes an abrupt turn, I try, like
Jesus, to hunker down on the edge of emptiness and pray.

Ezekiel 37:21–28
Jeremiah 31:10,11–12abcd,13
John 11:45–56

They brought the colt to Jesus
and put their cloaks over it.
And he sat on it.
Many people spread their cloaks on the road,
and others spread leafy branches
that they had cut from the fields.
Those preceding him as well as those following
kept crying out:
"Hosanna!
Blessed is he who comes in the name of the Lord!"
—MARK 11:7–9

I do not like huge crowds of people. Especially, I dislike crowds of shouting people. I wonder how the gentle healer and preacher felt atop the donkey as the branches waved and the cloaks were thrown down. Did he smile? Did he wave to his fickle supporters? Or did he look on the noisy, jostling crowd in sorrow and prayer?

PROCESSION:
Mark 11:1–10 or John 12:12–16

MASS:
Isaiah 50:4–7
Psalm 22:8–9,17–18,19–20,23–24
Philippians 2:6–11
Mark 14:1—15:47 or 15:1–39

Monday

MARCH 29

• MONDAY OF HOLY WEEK •

Then Judas the Iscariot, one of his disciples,
and the one who would betray him, said,
"Why was this oil not sold for three hundred
days' wages
and given to the poor?"
He said this not because he cared about the poor
but because he was a thief and held the money bag
and used to steal the contributions.
—JOHN 12:4–6,7

Not only is Judas a thief, but also he accuses other people of being wasteful with the money for the poor. He accuses Jesus, specifically, of being part of the problem. The people, agencies, and institutions that are most trying to help the poor are under constant scrutiny and suspicion. People say to me, "I don't know which charities are trustworthy." Charities are fallible like all humans, but accusing them of mismanagement is largely a distraction from the real thieves. Judas is an important person to ponder.

Isaiah 42:1–7
Psalm 27:1,2,3,13–14
John 12:1–11

Tuesday

MARCH 30

Jesus was deeply troubled and testified,
"Amen, amen, I say to you, one of you
will betray me."
The disciples looked at each other, at a loss
as to who he meant.
—JOHN 13:21–22

Jesus never did anything casually. He wouldn't have thrown off this hint without having a purpose in mind. Was he warning the apostles not to trust one another? Was he still hoping that Judas might reconsider the betrayal he had planned? Or, perhaps . . . is he warning us?

Isaiah 49:1–6
Psalm 71:1–2,3–4a,5ab–6ab,15 and 17
John 13:21–33,36–38

Wednesday

MARCH 31

• WEDNESDAY OF HOLY WEEK •

The Lord GOD has given me
a well-trained tongue,
That I might know how to speak to the weary
a word that will rouse them.
Morning after morning
he opens my ear that I may hear.
—Isaiah 50:4

The readings this week are so very heavy. Twice yesterday, I read through all of them for today and was overwhelmed by the dread of Jesus' coming passion. I gave up and went to bed, awoke this morning, and prayed as usual. And then, I came back to the lectionary and began to read the Scriptures again. I stopped at this first line and knew this was as far as I need go. Have I spoken a word to rouse the weary? Dear reader, is your heart lighter from following this book? This morning, God opened my ear, and I am listening for you. I pray it helps you rise.

Isaiah 50:4–9a
Psalm 69:8–10,21–22,31 and 33–34
Matthew 26:14–25

• THURSDAY OF HOLY WEEK (HOLY THURSDAY) •

Behold, he is coming amid the clouds,
and every eye will see him,
even those who pierced him.
All the peoples of the earth will lament him.
Yes. Amen.
—REVELATION 1:7

Holy Thursday is nearly as sad as Good Friday. The idea of a "last supper" tears my heart. This day is one long farewell. He told his apostles many times that he was going to die, and they argued with him, certain that it could be avoided. He also told them many times that he would return one day. It's wisdom not to argue with him. Accept the sadness, the goodbyes, and the hope. "Yes. Amen."

CHRISM MASS:
Isaiah 61:1–3a,6a,8b–9
Psalm 89:21–22,25,27
Revelation 1:5–8
Luke 4:16–21

EVENING MASS OF THE LORD'S SUPPER:
Exodus 12:1–8,11–14
Psalm 116:12–13,15–16bc,17–18
1 Corinthians 11:23–26
John 13:1–15

Friday

APRIL 2

*Standing by the cross of Jesus were his mother
and his mother's sister, Mary the wife of Clopas,
and Mary of Magdala.
When Jesus saw his mother and the disciple there
whom he loved,
he said to his mother, "Woman, behold, your son."
Then he said to the disciple,
"Behold, your mother."
And from that hour the disciple took her into his home.*
—JOHN 19:25–27

Hundreds of people were healed by him, thousands of people listened to him, and twelve followed him everywhere for three years. Yet these are the only ones who were at the foot of the cross when Jesus was dying. Once, someone told me, "There is always room at the foot of the cross."

Isaiah 52:13—53:12
Psalm 31:2,6,12–13,15–16,17,25
Hebrews 4;14–16; 5:7–9
John 18:1—19:42

Saturday

APRIL 3

If, then, we have died with Christ,
we believe that we shall also live with him.
—ROMANS 6:8

This is an if-then statement meaning, "If *this* happens, then *that* will happen," or "If *this* is true, then *that* is true as well." The second part of the phrase depends on the first part. This is important to understand. Read Romans 6:3–11, reflect on it, and ask God to show you in what way he wants you to die so that you can live with him.

VIGIL:
Genesis 1:1—2:2 or 1:26–31a
Psalm 104:1–2,5–6,10,12,13–14,24,35 or
33:4–5,6–7,12–13,20–22
Genesis 22:1–18 or 22:1–2,9a,10–13,15–18
Psalm 16:5,8,9–10,11
Exodus 14:15—15:1
Exodus 15:1–2,3–4,5–6,17–18
Isaiah 54:5–14
Psalm 30:2,4,5–6,11–12,13
Isaiah 55:1–11

Isaiah 12:2–3,4,5–6
Baruch 3:9–15,32—4:4
Psalm 19:8,9,10,11
Ezekiel 36:16–17a,18–28
Psalm 42:3,5; 43:3,4 or Isaiah
12:2–3,4bcd,5–6 or Psalm
51:12–13,14–15,18–19
Romans 6:3–11
Psalm 118:1–2,16–17,22–23
Mark 16:1–7

Sunday

APRIL 4

• EASTER SUNDAY OF THE RESURRECTION OF THE LORD •

On the first day of the week,
Mary of Magdala came to the tomb
early in the morning,
while it was still dark,
and saw the stone removed from the tomb.
—JOHN 20:1

Mary of Magdala went to the tomb before sunrise, "while it was still dark." She was a gutsy lady. She had stood at the foot of the cross, was there when Jesus was laid in the tomb, and absolutely everyone knew her as a follower of the crucified Nazarene. Yet Mary of Magdala went through the city in the dark. Her faith was great, and her love was even greater. Don't wait for daylight; look for Jesus while it is still dark.

Acts 10:34a,37–43
Psalm 118:1–2,16–17,22–23
Colossians 3:1–4 or 1 Corinthians 5:6b–8
John 20:1–9 or Mark 16:1–7 or, at an afternoon or evening Mass, Luke 24:13–35

Monday

APRIL 5

• MONDAY WITHIN THE OCTAVE OF EASTER •

Mary Magdalene and the other Mary went away
quickly from the tomb,
fearful yet overjoyed,
and ran to announce the news to his disciples.
And behold, Jesus met them on their way and
greeted them.
They approached, embraced his feet and did
him homage.
—MATTHEW 28:8–9

The two Marys are running to tell the disciples what the angel has told them, and Jesus meets them on the way. This happens often, Jesus meeting us on the way. Jesus met Paul on the way to Damascus. Jesus met the blind man on the road. Jesus meets us when we are going somewhere else. Look for him along the way.

Acts 2:14,22–33
Psalm 16:1–2a and 5,7–8,9–10,11
Matthew 28:8–15

Tuesday

APRIL 6

• TUESDAY WITHIN THE OCTAVE OF EASTER •

Jesus said to her, "Mary!"
She turned and said to him in Hebrew, "Rabbouni,"
which means Teacher.
Jesus said to her, "Stop holding on to me,
for I have not yet ascended to the Father.
But go to my brothers and tell them,
'I am going to my Father and your Father,
to my God and your God.'"
—JOHN 20:16–17

I, too, need to stop holding on to the man Jesus. He has gone to the Father: his and mine. I need to let go of his scarred feet and embrace his glory that is so bright it makes him unrecognizable to even his closest friends. The risen Christ is bigger than my own personal friend. He is that, still, but much more. He will do more in my life as my risen Lord than he could ever do walking the earth.

Acts 2:36–41
Psalm 33:4–5,18–19,20 and 22
John 20:11–18

Wednesday

APRIL 7

And he said to them, "Oh, how foolish you are!
How slow of heart to believe all the
prophets spoke!
Was it not necessary that the Christ should suffer
these things
and enter into his glory?"
—LUKE 24:25–26

Jesus is telling the disciples that they are in denial: They
don't believe the evidence in front of their eyes and the
predictions in the Scriptures. I wonder which evidence I am
refusing to believe? What is right in front of me yet I don't
want to acknowledge that God told us these things would
happen? The biggest thing I pretend not to see is Jesus'
promise that he would be with me always. If I really believed
this, I would never gossip, ignore the needy, or neglect to
pray. If I really believed that Jesus was standing next to me, I
would do my best to be a saint.

Acts 3:1–10
Psalm 105:1–2,3–4,6–7,8–9
Luke 24:13–35

Thursday

APRIL 8

The disciples of Jesus recounted what had taken
place along the way,
and how they had come to recognize him
in the breaking of the bread.

While they were still speaking about this,
he stood in their midst and said to them,
"Peace be with you."
But they were startled and terrified
and thought that they were seeing a ghost.
—LUKE 24:35–37

This strikes me as amusing. The disciples are telling each other about seeing the risen Christ, but then Jesus appears in front of them and they are immediately terrified. It's so much easier to talk *about* Jesus than to talk *to* Jesus.

Acts 3:11–26
Psalm 8:2ab and 5,6–7,8–9
Luke 24:35–48

Jesus said to them, "Come, have breakfast."
And none of the disciples dared to ask him,
"Who are you?"
because they realized it was the Lord.
Jesus came over and took the bread and gave it to them,
and in like manner the fish.
—JOHN 21:12–13

Jesus has compassion on the disciples, who are suffering
terrible guilt for having failed him so badly during his
passion. They know he is alive; he is sitting in front of them
on the beach, making breakfast. But they don't want to ask
any questions. If this were a normal reunion of friends, it
would be full of conversation and expressions of love.
Instead, they are staring at him, dumbfounded and
remorseful. Jesus understands their anxious emptiness. He
does the cooking and feeds them. He does the same for us
when we mess up.

Acts 4:1–12
Psalm 118:1–2 and 4,22–24,25–27a
John 21:1–14

Saturday

APRIL 10

*So they [the Sanhedrin] called them [Peter and John] back
and ordered them not to speak or teach at all
in the name of Jesus.
Peter and John, however, said to them in reply,
"Whether it is right in the sight of God
for us to obey you rather than God, you be the judges.
It is impossible for us not to speak about what we
have seen and heard."*
—ACTS 4:18–20

Yesterday, I met a woman who had recently rediscovered
God and religion. Tears shining in her eyes, she leaned
toward me to tell about the joy she felt in her new way of
living. I said to her, "I can see that you are on fire." Her face
brightened even more, and she nodded. "Exactly! I think
about it all the time." And, like Peter and John, it was
impossible for her not to speak of it.

Acts 4:13–21
Psalm 118:1 and 14–15ab,16–18,19–21
Mark 16:9–15

• SECOND SUNDAY OF EASTER (OR SUNDAY OF DIVINE MERCY) •

With great power the apostles bore witness
to the resurrection of the Lord Jesus,
and great favor was accorded them all.
—ACTS 4:33

This is not a time to waffle. Jesus' resurrection is not debatable. He either rose from the dead after public torture and execution or our faith is silly. If we speak about Jesus "with great power," then Jesus' love will go out through us into the world. Today, just one time, look someone in the eye and say, "Jesus was killed and was buried. Three days later, he came back to life, completely well. I know this is true." If you can do this, you will not regret it.

Acts 4:32–35
Psalm 118:2–4,13–15,22–24
1 John 5:1–6
John 20:19–31

Monday

APRIL 12

*As they prayed, the place where they were
gathered shook,
and they were all filled with the Holy Spirit
and continued to speak the word of God
with boldness.*

—ACTS 4:31

This excerpt from The Acts of the Apostles is not about
Pentecost; that happened back in section 2. This is another
time that the Holy Spirit arrived and shook the believers.
And it will happen again and again in the subsequent
sections. Thousands of people will be converted, and the
believers will preach and love and be brave in the face of
persecution. It seems to happen when the people gather and
pray together. Our lesson might be this: if we don't want the
Holy Spirit to shake things up, we should probably not
gather and pray.

Acts 4:23–31
Psalm 2:1–3,4–7a,7b–9
John 3:1–8

Tuesday

APRIL 13

• ST. MARTIN I, POPE AND MARTYR •

The community of believers was of one heart and mind,
and no one claimed that any of his possessions
was his own,
but they had everything in common.
With great power the Apostles bore witness
to the resurrection of the Lord Jesus,
and great favor was accorded them all.
—ACTS 4:32–33

Power does not come from the people but from God working in the people. It is false humility and a temptation to say, "We are so small, so poor, so unworthy, so powerless that we cannot do the wonderful things described in The Acts of the Apostles." People do not do those wonders; God does the wonders. We need to believe in God, not in ourselves. We limit God's works by not being "of one heart and mind."

Acts 4:32–37
Psalm 93:1ab,1cd–2,5
John 3:7b–15

The high priest rose up and all his companions,
that is, the party of the Sadducees,
and, filled with jealousy,
laid hands upon the Apostles and put them
in the public jail.
—ACTS 5:17–18

Spiritual jealousy is a sin of pride. We want to be holy, yet if we see someone whom others deem holier than we are, we seize them, put them on trial, and silence them. When he looks at the splintering of the Christian churches, God must be holding his head with both hands.

Acts 5:17–26
Psalm 34:2–3,4–5,6–7,8–9
John 3:16–21

*When the court officer had brought the Apostles in
and made them stand before the Sanhedrin,
the high priest questioned them,
"We gave you strict orders did we not,
to stop teaching in that name.
Yet you have filled Jerusalem with your teaching
and want to bring this man's blood upon us."*
—ACTS 5:27–28

The unauthorized Jesus freaks are dragged again and again
before the religious leaders to be scolded, threatened, and
abused. Then, as soon as they are released, they go right
back out and preach Jesus' name. This is the basic plot of all
reform movements. I pay attention when a layperson, a nun,
or a cleric gets up and starts talking about Jesus. It's important
to note if they are talking about Jesus or about something
else. If they are talking about something else, I stop paying
attention.

Acts 5:27–33
Psalm 34:2,9,17–18,19–20
John 3:31–36

Friday
APRIL 16

[Rabbi Gamaliel speaking to the Sanhedrin] "So now I tell you,
have nothing to do with these men, and let them go.
For if this endeavor or this activity is of human origin,
it will destroy itself.
But if it comes from God, you will not be able
to destroy them;
you may even find yourselves fighting against God."
They were persuaded by him.
—ACTS 5:38–39

I try to remember this story when one of my well-intended
efforts to serve God fails miserably. At times, I forget that I
am God's servant, not the other way around. My great ideas
and plans are not God's plans. In fact, my plans may be
working at cross-purposes with God's, just like the
Sanhedrin's plans to destroy the Jesus movement.

Acts 5:34–42
Psalm 27:1,4,13–14
John 6:1–15

As the number of disciples continued to grow,
the Hellenists complained against the Hebrews
because their widows
were being neglected in the daily distribution.

—ACTS 6:1

I have belonged to several different church groups over the
years, and this story sounds like a typical scenario. People
lose their generosity when they think there isn't enough.
St. Vincent de Paul said, "Take care not to tread on the heels
of Providence." I try to remind myself that God provides all
we need, when we need it. Stepping on God's heels and
pushing from behind shows a lack of trust. The Hebrew
Christians thought there was only enough for their widows
and not for the Greek widows. Their lack of faith was
showing.

Acts 6:1–7
Psalm 33:1–2,4–5,18–19
John 6:16–21

"The author of life you put to death,
but God raised him from the dead;
of this we are witnesses.
Now I know, brothers, that you acted out of ignorance, just as your
leaders did; but God has thus brought to fulfillment what he had
announced beforehand through the mouth of all the prophets, that his
Christ would suffer. Repent, therefore, and be converted, that your sins
may be wiped away."
—ACTS 3:15,17–19

Peter is talking to the same people who yelled, "Crucify him!"
only a short time before. This speech is mercy itself. Not
only is there no talk of revenge, but all he asks for is
repentance, and he promises that their sins will be wiped
away. Peter has received mercy. Peter understands the deep,
deep holiness of mercy. Lord, help me to be merciful.

Acts 3:13–15,17–19
Psalm 4:2,4,7–8,9(7a)
1 John 2:1–5a
Luke 24:35–48

Remove from me the way of falsehood,
and favor me with your law.
The way of truth I have chosen;
I have set your ordinances before me.
—PSALM 119:29–30

In today's Gospel, Pilate says to Jesus, "What is truth?" Sounds like the most cynical question ever asked. Pilate did not want to know the truth; he wanted to know the way out of what he saw as a no-win decision. In Psalm 119, the poet is not asking to know the truth but is choosing to follow the "way of truth." Perhaps, with our limited knowledge of hearts, we will never be able to know the entire truth of the matters concerning us. Like Pilate, we might see no-win choices in front of us. While the psalmist wrote about God's ordinances as the way of truth, Jesus said, "I am the way, the truth, and the life." If Pilate had only known. . . .

Acts 6:8–15
Psalm 119:23–24,26–27,29–30
John 6:22–29

Stephen said to the people, the elders, and the scribes:
"You stiff-necked people, uncircumcised in heart
and ears,
you always oppose the Holy Spirit;
you are just like your ancestors."
—ACTS 7:51

Stephen is a harsh critic. He insults his opposition by calling
them "uncircumcised"—in other words, not true Jews. He
accuses them of battling against the very spirit of God, and
he expands that to include their ancestors. Stephen uses
absolute language like "you always" and "you are just like,"
the kind of name-calling that is sure to rile people up. He has
no nuance, diplomacy, or consideration for people's feelings.
I don't argue about religion with people, not because I'm
afraid of being stoned but because it would be worse to be
throwing the stones—far worse. When insulted, I have it in
me to throw stones.

Acts 7:51—8:1a
Psalm 31:3cd–4,6 and 7b and 8a,17 and 21ab
John 6:30–35

⇒ 143 ⇐

*There broke out a severe persecution of the Church in Jerusalem,
and all were scattered throughout the countryside of Judea and Samaria,
except the Apostles. Devout men buried Stephen and made a loud lament
over him. Saul, meanwhile, was trying to destroy the Church; entering
house after house and dragging out men and women, he handed them over
for imprisonment.*

—ACTS 8:1B–3

This is a description of the persecuted Church. It sounds
dreadful and scary. When people use the word *persecution* to
describe the way the church is treated in our society, I get a
little bored. We sound fearful, as if we don't have God to
protect us. Others see through this hype. No one is stoning
us or dragging us out of our houses to be jailed. We must be
careful with our words and respect people who truly are
persecuted; otherwise, our words lose their meaning.

Acts 8:1b–8
Psalm 66:1–3a,4–5,6–7a
John 6:35–40

As they traveled along the road
they came to some water,
and the eunuch said, "Look, there is water.
What is to prevent my being baptized?"
—ACTS 8:36

"I am the living bread that came down from heaven;
whoever eats this bread will live forever;
and the bread that I will give
is my Flesh for the life of the world."
—JOHN 6:51

I chose two verses today because they both provoked the same longing in me. "What is to prevent my being baptized?" and "whoever eats this bread will live forever" sound to me as if God is saying, "What are you protecting? Look, there is water. Look, there is bread. Be baptized. Take and eat." I hold God's grace hostage when I do not partake of it and when I refuse to share it.

Acts 8:26–40
Psalm 66:8–9,16–17,20
John 6:44–51

He [Paul] stayed some days with the disciples in Damascus,
and he began at once to proclaim Jesus
in the synagogues,
that he is the Son of God.
—ACTS 9:19B–20

Paul isn't just a little converted—he is extremely converted. After "breathing murderous threats against the disciples," he meets Jesus on the road, and everything he previously believed crumbles. "At once" he starts to preach that Jesus is the Son of God. Most of us take longer than this to change our minds, to grow to trust Jesus instead of our own ideas and certainty. Not Paul; he truly shows us how to throw off our old selves, old friends, and false teachers and to believe in mercy instead.

Acts 9:1–20
Psalm 117:1bc,2
John 6:52–59

Saturday

APRIL 24

• ST. FIDELIS OF SIGMARINGEN, PRIEST AND MARTYR •

*Jesus then said to the Twelve, "Do you also want
to leave?"
Simon Peter answered him, "Master, to whom shall
we go?
You have the words of eternal life.
We have come to believe
and are convinced that you are the Holy One
of God."*
—JOHN 6:67–69

What Catholic hasn't had the temptation to leave the church
in the past few years? The scandals have been increasingly
mortifying and faith-shaking. We are all suspected of being
either child molesters or conspirers to cover it up. People ask
us, "Why are you still going to church?" In our depression
and confusion, the only answer we have is Peter's: we have
come to believe and are convinced that Jesus is the Holy
One of God.

Acts 9:31–42
Psalm 116:12–13,14–15,16–17
John 6:60–69

Sunday

APRIL 25

• FOURTH SUNDAY OF EASTER •

Jesus said:
"I am the good shepherd.
A good shepherd lays down his life for the sheep.
A hired man, who is not a shepherd
and whose sheep are not his own,
sees a wolf coming and leaves the sheep and runs away,
and the wolf catches and scatters them."
—JOHN 10:11–12

Who does this? Who lays down their life for someone other than a family member? Obviously, soldiers, police officers, and firefighters do this for the citizenry they protect. In recent years during school shootings, many teachers and administrators have died for their students. Nurses, doctors, and hospital staff often stay at their work during hurricanes, tsunamis, earthquakes, and wildfires in order to evacuate patients. Pilots, captains, and attendants remain onboard until passengers are off. Jesus is saying, "I won't leave you. I'll stay until you're safe or we go to heaven together."

Acts 4:8–12
Psalm 118:1,8–9,21–23,26,28,29(22)
1 John 3:1–2
John 10:11–18

Monday

APRIL 26

Athirst is my soul for God, the living God.
When shall I go and behold the face of God?
—PSALM 42:3

As we age, we don't notice when we are thirsty. My doctor
tells me to drink more water, to make a point of it, not to
wait until I feel thirsty. I wonder if this is true of spiritual
thirst as well? As we age, as life changes, do we forget to
thirst for the face of God? Do we think that God's wisdom is
something we can drink when we wake in the morning and
then neglect the rest of the day? Is half a cupful enough? Can
we just sip on coffee and other stimulants and count that as
hydration? No. We can't just sip on a few Scriptures and tidy
prayers, either. As we age, we need to remember to drink of
God more often than before.

Acts 11:1–18
Psalm 42:2–3; 43:3–4
John 10:1–10

⇒ 149 ⇐

Tuesday

APRIL 27

*And Jesus walked about in the temple area on
the Portico of Solomon.
So the Jews gathered around him and said to him,
"How long are you going to keep us in suspense?
If you are the Christ, tell us plainly."
Jesus answered them, "I told you and you do not believe.
The works I do in my Father's name testify to me."*
—JOHN 10:23–25

Sometimes I wonder: If I stay on the fence too long, will
Jesus' words seem more and more vague? Will I insist that
God hasn't properly revealed himself and it's his fault that my
faith is so uncertain? "Jesus walked about in the temple area":
Will I tell God that he is too hard to find, while refusing to
look for him where he usually hangs out among the poor?
On my deathbed, will I complain that Jesus kept me in
suspense?

Acts 11:19–26
Psalm 87:1b–3,4–5,6–7
John 10:22–30

Wednesday
APRIL 28

The word of God continued to spread and grow.
—ACTS 12:24

This verse in Acts follows the story of Peter's escape and Herod's furious anger and sudden death. It negates our expectation that the word of God might spread in a nice, orderly fashion, with scheduled meetings, creative workbooks, and calm discussions. If I'm reading it correctly, according to Acts, the word of God spreads through fervent prayer, courage, risk, opposition, and unquenchable joy and faith.

Acts 12:24—13:5a
Psalm 67:2–3,5,6 and 8
John 12:44–50

When Jesus had washed the disciples' feet,
he said to them:
"Amen, amen, I say to you, no slave is greater
than his master
nor any messenger greater than the one
who sent him.
If you understand this, blessed are you if you do it."
—JOHN 13:16–17

One time, on a St. Vincent de Paul home visit with my husband to the apartment of an elderly couple, the gentleman was worried about his foot, which had swollen and turned red. He asked us to look at it. I thought this was not such a good idea, but Dean knelt down and gently removed the man's sock. He didn't touch the sore spot, only looked and commiserated. "If you think you should see a doctor, I think so too," he said. St. Vincent told us that the poor are our masters. Jesus says, "No slave is greater than his master."

Acts 13:13–25
Psalm 89:2–3,21–22,25 and 27
John 13:16–20

Friday

APRIL 30

• ST. PIUS V, POPE •

Jesus said to him, "I am the way and the truth and the life."
—JOHN 14:6

Today, take this well-known self-definition of Jesus and substitute synonyms.

The way: the path, the direction, the twists and turns, the method, the map, the instructions.

The truth: the facts, the reality, the undeniable, the unchangeable.

The life: animation, breath, sustenance, fragility, strength, existence, interdependence, independence, organism.

"I am the twist and turns, the reality, and the breath."

Now, choose your own.

Acts 13:26–33
Psalm 2:6–7,8–9,10–11ab
John 14:1–6

Saturday

MAY 1

• ST. JOSEPH THE WORKER •

"Amen, amen, I say to you,
whoever believes in me will do the works that I do,
and will do greater ones than these,
because I am going to the Father.
And whatever you ask in my name, I will do,
so that the Father may be glorified in the Son."
—JOHN 14:12–13

My fellow Vincentians were on a home visit in the house of a
middle-aged woman who couldn't work because of a back
injury. They listened to her story, went through her budget
item by item, and helped her find other sources of assistance
from the community. Then they offered to pay her mortgage
until the expected unemployment payments would begin.
Her first reaction was to look above their heads to the cross
hanging on her wall. Instantly, they knew she was seeing
God's works, not theirs. Through them, Jesus had answered
her prayers, and God was glorified.

Acts 13:44–52
Psalm 98:1,2–3ab,3cd–4
John 14:7–14 or Matthew 13:54–58

───────

⇒ 154 ⇐

Sunday

MAY 2

"I am the vine, you are the branches.
Whoever remains in me and I in him will bear much fruit,
because without me you can do nothing."
—JOHN 15:5

We all know that we can do a lot of stuff without even giving
a thought to Jesus or to what Jesus wants us to be doing.
Keeping busy is always possible. *Bearing fruit* with our
constant activity is another thing altogether. Jesus tells the
branches to stay attached, allow themselves to be pruned, be
simple, bloom, let the sap flow, and bend under the weight of
the fruit. How do we remember to slow down and be a
branch? Branches turn to the light and cling to the vine: in
other words—pray and trust.

Acts 9:26–31
Psalm 22:26–27,28,30,31–32(26a)
1 John 3:18–24
John 15:1–8

Monday

MAY 3

*After that he [the risen Jesus] appeared to more
than five hundred brothers and sisters at once,
most of whom are still living,
though some have fallen asleep.
After that he appeared to James,
then to all the Apostles.*
—1 CORINTHIANS 15:6–7

Can you imagine the turmoil in Jerusalem with five hundred
people claiming they have seen the resurrected Christ?
Everyone in town must have been able to hear an eyewitness
account from a friend or family member. If five hundred
people in any town suddenly claimed they had seen an
executed person come back to life, it would be plain
stubbornness to remain incredulous.

1 Corinthians 15:1–8
Psalm 19:2–3,4–5
John 14:6–14

Tuesday

MAY 4

Jesus said to his disciples:
"Peace I leave with you; my peace I give to you.
Not as the world gives do I give it to you.
Do not let your hearts be troubled or afraid."
—JOHN 14:27

Jesus has given us a definition of his peace by pointing to *something that it is not.* So, what is the world's peace like? It is usually defined by an absence of war. Jesus' peace is not like that. Sometimes the world's peace means that everyone has stockpiled weapons, and peace is kept because the nations are afraid of mutual annihilation. Jesus' peace isn't like that, either. The world can be at peace when only one person or country is in charge and dissension is not tolerated. Jesus doesn't give that kind of peace either.

Acts 14:19–28
Psalm 145:10–11,12–13ab,21
John 14:27–31a

⇒ 157 ⇐

Wednesday

MAY 5

*Some who had come down from Judea were instructing the brothers,
"Unless you are circumcised according to the Mosaic practice, you
cannot be saved." Because there arose no little dissension and debate by
Paul and Barnabas with them, it was decided that Paul, Barnabas, and
some of the others should go up to Jerusalem to the Apostles and
presbyters about this question.*
—ACTS 15:1–2

Today and tomorrow, Acts 15 tells the story of the Council of
Jerusalem, or the Apostolic Council, in about the year 50.
There were disagreement, debate, silent listening, and
speeches, and afterward a consensus was reached to make it
fairly simple for people who desired to join the faith. There
were rules but not hundreds, or even dozens, of them—only a
few rules. They wanted people to join the church more than
they wanted control.

Acts 15:1–6
Psalm 122:1–2,3–4ab,4cd–5
John 15:1–8

Thursday

MAY 6

"If you keep my commandments, you will remain
in my love,
just as I have kept my Father's commandments
and remain in his love.

"I have told you this so that
my joy might be in you and
your joy might be complete."
—JOHN 15:10–11

Let's think about joy. We don't achieve it or earn it. Joy is something that comes over us. It happens to us: when we find out a baby is coming, or a person we love is healed, or we are reunited with loved ones, or a simple sunrise brings tears to our eyes. Keeping God's commandments will not bring joy. God brings joy. God comes when we obey his commandments of loving him and loving our neighbor.

Acts 15:7–21
Psalm 96:1–2a,2b–3,10
John 15:9–11

"This I command you: love one another."
—JOHN 15:17

As I read Jesus' words today, I wonder how he thought his command to "love one another" was going to work out. Jesus commanded us to love, but it's our decision to give love. His gift of free will is a forever gift. He knew that each and every day some of us would disobey.

Acts 15:22–31
Psalm 57:8–9,10 and 12
John 15:12–17

Saturday

MAY 8

Sing joyfully to the LORD, all you lands;
serve the LORD with gladness;
come before him with joyful song.
—PSALM 100:1B–2

Sneering, pessimistic, fearful Christians are an oxymoron. Joy comes from knowing and loving Jesus, and God who sent him. Whenever I sense fear seeping into my thoughts, I try to remind myself that I gave that up for Lent.

Acts 16:1–10
Psalm 100:1b–2,3,5
John 15:18–21

Beloved, let us love one another,
because love is of God;
everyone who loves is begotten by God and knows God.
Whoever is without love does not know God,
for God is love.
—1 JOHN 4:7–8

Picture that a letter arrives in your mailbox today. It's from someone named John, but you know many Johns. You open it and read several pages telling you how much God loves you. Then there are reminders that hating people is not love, followed by explanations of how love is recognized in actions. As you turn over the sheets of paper, the writer reveals that you are actually one of God's beloved children. He tells you that you and God can conquer the world. At this point, you put down the letter and look again at the address on the envelope. You are thinking, *Is this really for me?* Yes. It is.

Acts 10:25–26,34–35,44–48
Psalm 98:1,2–3,3–4 (See 2b.)
1 John 4:7–10
John 15:9–17

Monday

MAY 10

*We set sail from Troas, making a straight run
for Samothrace,
and on the next day to Neapolis,
and from there to Philippi,
a leading city in that district of Macedonia
and a Roman colony.*
—ACTS 16:11–12A

Paul and his companions traveled extensively to bring Jesus to as many people as possible. St. Damien de Veuster of Molokai (1840–1889) traveled all the way from his native Belgium to the Hawaiian Islands to do the same thing. He volunteered to serve the people suffering from leprosy on the island of Molokai and, after sixteen years, succumbed to the disease himself. During those years, Fr. Damien lifted both the spirits and the living conditions of the colony. He brought government support and an order of Sisters to assist with the work. During his life, all called him either "a saint" or "a fool." It's often difficult to tell the difference.

Acts 16:11–15
Psalm 149:1b–2,3–4,5–6a and 9b
John 15:26—16:4a

*He put them in the innermost cell
and secured their feet to a stake.*

*About midnight, while Paul and Silas were praying
and singing hymns to God as the prisoners listened,
there was suddenly such a severe earthquake
that the foundations of the jail shook;
all the doors flew open, and the chains of all
were pulled loose.*
—ACTS 16:24B–26

This sounds like a terrifying incident. The jailer was certainly frightened enough to become an instant convert. Paul, on the other hand, appears unruffled. He goes straight on praying, singing hymns, and preaching the gospel. Paul's foundations are not shaken as the foundations of the jail are. Paul depends on the foundation of Jesus and on nothing else.

Acts 16:22–34
Psalm 138:1–2ab,2cde–3,7c–8
John 16:5–11

Wednesday

MAY 12

Jesus said to his disciples:
"I have much more to tell you, but you cannot
bear it now.
But when he comes, the Spirit of truth,
he will guide you to all truth."

—JOHN 16:12

This passage is part of the Last Supper discourse. I wonder what further truth Jesus had to tell the disciples that they couldn't bear at that moment? He had already told them several times that he was going to die. He had warned them that they would have to give up everything to follow him. He had taught them for three years. I sometimes wonder if The Acts of the Apostles, the letters of Paul, and the visions of saints are all parts of this truth. The sacrifices of martyrs, the futile attempts to teach the incredulous, and the splintering of the church are certainly all unbearable as well. We were not created strong enough to know the future.

Acts 17:15,22—18:1
Psalm 148:1–2,11–12,13,14
John 16:12–15

Thursday

MAY  13

*Amen, amen, I say to you, you will weep and mourn, while the world
rejoices; you will grieve, but your grief will become joy.*

—JOHN 16:20

Grieving is part of our life as people of faith. Sometimes
mourning is appropriate and necessary. And, often, we grieve
over sins and ills that the world considers insignificant. We
are expressing God's heart.

Acts 18:1–8
Psalm 98:1,2–3ab,3cd–4
John 16:16–20
In some regions of the USA, this day celebrates the Ascension of the Lord.
See readings for May 16.

Friday

MAY 14

• ST. MATTHIAS, APOSTLE •

"I have told you this so that my joy be in you
and your joy might be complete.
This is my commandment: love one another
as I love you."
—JOHN 15:11–12

Jesus must have exuded joy. I picture him with twinkling eyes
and a ready smile. Children were attracted to him, so much
so that the apostles had to shoo them away. Children are not
attracted to glum people. When Jesus cured the sick, which
was often, shouts of joy and exclamation must have taken
over the situation. Jesus surely would have joined in the
celebrations with his own laughter and tears of joy. To gain
this joy, we need only to love people as Jesus loved people.
Lord, I thirst for your joy. Let me begin again today to love
with your love.

Acts 1:15–17,20–26
Psalm 113:1–2,3–4,5–6,7–8
John 15:9–17

Saturday

MAY 15

• ST. ISIDORE •

A Jew named Apollos, a native of Alexandria, an eloquent speaker,
arrived in Ephesus. He was an authority on the Scriptures. He had been
instructed in the Way of the Lord and, with ardent spirit, spoke and
taught accurately about Jesus, although he knew only the baptism of
John. He began to speak boldly in the synagogue; but when Priscilla
and Aquila heard him, they took him aside and explained to him the
Way of God more accurately. And when he wanted to cross to Achaia,
the brothers encouraged him and wrote to the disciples there to
welcome him.

—ACTS 18:24–27A

Clearly, I am not an authority on the Scriptures. I do possess an
"ardent spirit" for Jesus, and through the encouragement of
other believers I am writing these words. These others, like
Priscilla and Aquila, take me aside and explain God's ways to
me. I am grateful, so very grateful.

Acts 18:23–28
Psalm 47:2–3,8–9,10
John 16:23b–28

⇒ 168 ⇐

Sunday

MAY 16

• THE ASCENSION OF THE LORD • SEVENTH SUNDAY OF EASTER •

While they were looking intently at the sky
as he was going,
suddenly two men dressed in white garments
stood beside them.
They said, "Men of Galilee,
why are you standing there looking at the sky?
This Jesus who has been taken up from you into heaven
will return in the same way as you have seen him
going into heaven."
—ACTS 1:10–11

Are the two men dressed in white saying, "Stop standing around. Get to work," or are they saying, "Jesus is coming back, but it will be in a spectacular way"? Perhaps both.

Acts 1:1–11
Psalm 47:2–3,6–7,8–9
Ephesians 1:17–23 or 4:1–13 or 4:1–7,11–13
Mark 16:15–20

Monday

MAY 17

"In the world you will have trouble,
but take courage, I have conquered the world."
—JOHN 16:33

Jesus never promised us an easy path. Life is what it is: good,
bad, beautiful, ugly. Jesus tells us to take courage in times of
trouble because it is our faith in him that will transform those
very same troubles into instruments of God. Life will have
troubles; that is the truth. Faith makes those troubles work
for God.

Acts 19:1–8
Psalm 68:2–3ab,4–5acd,6–7ab
John 16:29–33

"Now this is eternal life,
that they should know you, the only true God,
and the one whom you sent, Jesus Christ."
—JOHN 17:3

Jesus seems to be saying that eternal life is knowing God and
Jesus. Wait. If this is the definition of eternal life, then we
can be experiencing eternity here and now. All that is
required is that we know God. Of course, none of us can
know God and Jesus completely on this earth. Who can
know the mind of God? His ways are not our ways. It might
be like an algebraic function that *approaches* infinity but never
quite reaches it: a curved line that always increases yet never
finds an ending. By drawing close to Jesus, we are drawing
close to eternal life.

Acts 20:17–27
Psalm 68:10–11,20–21
John 17:1–11a

Wednesday

MAY 19

"But now I am coming to you.
I speak this in the world
so that they may share my joy completely."
—JOHN 17:13

This is part of a long goodbye prayer that Jesus is making before he begins his passion. Yet he is talking about sharing his joy. Not his distress, but joy. Have you ever heard the farewell song "The Parting Glass"? It's sung in pubs and tells the story of the first to leave a group of friends. Like Jesus, it speaks of joy. And it is also one of the most popular songs for funerals. Listen to the version with lyrics by Ed Sheeran on YouTube and imagine Jesus singing it to his friends. You are either one of his "comrades" or his "sweethearts." Believe it.

Acts 20:28–38
Psalm 68:29–30,33–35a,35bc–36ab
John 17:11b–19

Thursday

MAY 20

• ST. BERNARDINE OF SIENA, PRIEST •

Paul was aware that some were Sadducees
and some Pharisees,
so he called out before the Sanhedrin,
"My brothers, I am a Pharisee, the son of Pharisees;
I am on trial for hope in the resurrection of the dead."
When he said this,
a dispute broke out between the Pharisees
and Sadducees,
and the group became divided.
—ACTS 23:6–7

Paul knew very well how to divide his enemies. All he had to
do was bring up a matter of disputed doctrine, and the
opposition split and attacked each other instead of him. It is
foolish of us—we who study this Scripture—to let anyone
divide us along doctrinal lines. Jesus prayed to God to keep
us "one" and warned us that a house divided cannot stand. It's
okay to have differences of opinion on doctrine. It is not
okay to be divided over them.

Acts 22:30, 23:6–11
Psalm 16:1–2a and 5,7–8,9–10,11
John 17:20–26

Friday

MAY 21

For as the heavens are high above the earth,
so surpassing is his kindness toward those who fear him.
As far as the east is from the west,
so far has he put our transgressions from us.
—PSALM 103:11–12

The Gospel reading today is about Jesus asking Peter if he loves him. Jesus asks him three times and then tells Peter to follow him. The psalmist confirms that God is kind and forgiving. It's really, really important for us to believe in God's forgiveness. On our own, we are not strong enough to follow Jesus; we need to be certain that he loves us and forgives us completely. Jesus forgave Peter. Believe that he forgave you, as well. Don't doubt his mercy.

Acts 25:13b–21
Psalm 103:1–2,11–12,19–20ab
John 21:15–19

⇒ 174 ⇐

There are also many other things that Jesus did,
but if these were to be described individually,
I do not think the whole world would contain
the books
that would be written.
—JOHN 21:25

This last verse of John's Gospel tells me that we haven't yet received all Jesus' blessings. "There are also many other things that Jesus did," so someday, God willing, we will meet Jesus in eternity, and he will tell us the rest of the story. There are books and books of stories that we will receive. And, perhaps, one of those stories will be the story of our own life.

Acts 28:16–20,30–31
Psalm 11:4,5 and 7
John 21:20–25

Sunday

MAY 23

• PENTECOST SUNDAY •

Jesus said to them again, "Peace be with you.
As the Father has sent me, so I send you."
And when he had said this, he breathed on them
and said to them,
"Receive the Holy Spirit."
—JOHN 20:21–22

He said, "Receive the Holy Spirit." Not, "If you work hard,
the Holy Spirit will come to you." Not, "Understand the
Holy Spirit." Not, "Study the Holy Spirit." Not even,
"Worship the Holy Spirit." Simply stand there, or sit still, or
rest your weary head, *and receive.* Oh! Happy Pentecost!

VIGIL:
Genesis 11:1–9 or Exodus 19:3–8a,16–20b
or Ezekiel 37:1–4 or Joel 3:1–5
Psalm 104:1–2,24,35,27–28,29,30
Romans 8:22–27
John 7:37–39

DAY:
Acts 2:1–11
Psalm 104:1,24,29–30,31,34
1 Corinthians 12:3b–7,12–13 or
Galatians 5:16–25
John 20:19–23 or 15:26–27; 16:12–15

EXTENDED VIGIL:
Genesis 11:1–9
Psalm 33:10–11,12–13,14–15
Exodus 19:3–8a,16–20b
Daniel 3:52,53,54,55,56 or Psalm
19:8,9,10,11
Ezekiel 37:1–14
Psalm 107:2–3,4–5,6–7,8–9
Joel 3:1–5
Psalm 104:1–2,24, and 35,27–28,29–30
Romans 8:22–27
John 7:37–39

MAY  24

• THE BLESSED VIRGIN MARY, MOTHER OF THE CHURCH •

All these devoted themselves with one accord to prayer,
together with some women,
and Mary the mother of Jesus, and his brothers.
—ACTS 1:14

After Jesus' ascension, the apostles go back to the upper room to pray. Mary is with them along with "some women . . . and his brothers." This is the first congregation of our faith. I look around the pews in my home parish, and the place contains nearly the same types of people. The apostles are there in the presiders, and there are plenty of women and brothers. The difference is in the children. We have children praying with us now. The children are a sign that the church is still growing. If we reach a point where they are not present, then it probably means we are back in that upper room, afraid, and feeling the loss of Jesus. That is when we need Mary the most.

Genesis 3:9–15,20 or Acts 1:12–14
Psalm 87:1–2,3 and 5,6–7
John 19:25–34

• ST. BEDE THE VENERABLE, PRIEST AND DOCTOR OF THE CHURCH •
ST. GREGORY VII, POPE • ST. MARY MAGDALENE DE' PAZZI, VIRGIN •

In a generous spirit pay homage to the LORD,
be not sparing of freewill gifts.
With each contribution show a cheerful countenance,
and pay your tithes in a spirit of joy.
Give to the Most High as he has given to you,
generously, according to your means.
—SIRACH 35:10–12

Joy is a gift from God that is especially appropriate for two occasions: receiving and giving. Joy comes to us when we are aware of God's generous gifts to us: when we have our loved ones around us, when we breathe deeply in good health, and when we feel his forgiveness. If we give generously and freely, joy can also be present in us. We can ruin our giving if we do it with anxiety or resentment.

Sirach 35:1–12
Psalm 50:5–6,7–8,14 and 23
Mark 10:28–31

Wednesday

MAY 26

• ST. PHILIP NERI, PRIEST •

"Whoever wishes to be great among you will be
your servant;
whoever wishes to be first among you
will be the slave of all."
—MARK 10:43–44

One summer, for two days each week, I was a housekeeper for two families. I learned that serving is different from working as an employee at a business. Once, when the homeowner told me to clean out a bedroom, she said, "Take care not to slam the door because the shotgun leaning behind it is loaded." Any day, if she decided that she didn't need me, I didn't work, and I wasn't paid. Both families paid in cash and didn't contribute Social Security taxes, so I had to pay all the taxes myself. There was no break time, but they did allow me to eat my sack lunch. Read the quote from Mark again and think about what it actually means to be a servant.

Sirach 36:1,4–5a,10–17
Psalm 79:8,9,11 and 13
Mark 10:32–45

Thursday

MAY 27

*Jesus said to him in reply, "What do you want me to
do for you?"
The blind man replied to him, "Master, I want to see."*
—MARK 10:51

Jesus must have loved this request because he answered it
straight away and Bartimaeus was healed. I look and look at
the blind man's "prayer" and wonder what is in those five
words: *Master, I want to see. Master:* Bartimaeus recognizes Jesus
as the one in charge. *I want:* the blind man does not say
whatever you want but plainly answers Jesus' question, *What do
you want me to do for you?* Jesus invites him to ask. *To see:*
Bartimaeus asks big: he asks for something that only Jesus can
give with the power that he believes Jesus possesses.
Bartimaeus uses the power that he, himself, possesses: the
power of his faith in Jesus.

Sirach 42:15–25
Psalm 33:2–3,4–5,6–7,8–9
Mark 10:46–52

⇒ 180 ⇐

Then he taught them saying, "Is it not written:
My house shall be called a house of prayer for all peoples?
But you have made it a den of thieves."
—MARK 11:17

Jesus is quoting both Isaiah 56:7 and Jeremiah 7:11. And
now, here we have these words in Mark. They must be
important. Is my church a house of prayer for all people? Do
we buy and sell on the premises to profit ourselves?

Sirach 44:1,9–13
Psalm 149:1b–2,3–4,5–6a and 9b
Mark 11:11–26

Saturday

MAY 29

In the short time I paid heed,
I met with great instruction.
—SIRACH 51:16

Many Bible verses like this one make me cringe and laugh at
myself. God will give us great instruction when we pay heed.
It is just so hard to pay attention for more than a few
minutes! During any ordinary day, whatever I am busy with, I
so easily forget to pay attention to God. It means that I am
missing out on great instructions. Fortunately, God is a
patient teacher.

Sirach 51:12cd–20
Psalm 19:8,9,10,11
Mark 11:27–33

*"Go, therefore, and make disciples of all nations,
baptizing them in the name of the Father,
and of the Son, and of the Holy Spirit."*
—MATTHEW 28:19

I make the sign of the cross before I begin a meal, naming the Holy Trinity as I touch my head, chest, and shoulders. I also do this before I begin to write, while the computer is warming up. Baseball players have been known to do it before they step up to the plate to bat. Parents bless their children at bedtime. And, of course, there are all the times we do this during the Mass and other sacraments. Perhaps the Holy Trinity is as close as our fingertips and as everyday as food, work, play, children, and worship.

Deuteronomy 4:32–34,39–40
Psalm 33:4–5,6,9,18–19,20,22(12b)
Romans 8:14–17
Matthew 28:16–20

"He has come to the help of his servant Israel."
—LUKE 1:54

Mary is proclaiming her beautiful Magnificat, taking no
credit for herself and praising God in wonder and joy. Near
the end she says this line about God coming to the help of
his servant Israel. God comes down to help. We don't have to
reach up, because he will reach down. The entire Jesus story
is about God's humility. No wonder God loves Mary so
much. They are two peas in a pod, those two.

Zephaniah 3:14–18a or Romans 12:9–16
Isaiah 12:2–3,4bcd,5–6
Luke 1:39–56

*She said to me, "It was given to me as a bonus over
and above my wages."
Yet I would not believe her,
and told her to give it back to its owners.
I became very angry with her over this.
So she retorted: "Where are your charitable deeds now?
Where are your virtuous acts?
See! Your true character is finally showing itself!"*
—TOBIT 2:14

Tobit has turned blind, and his wife is earning the wages for
the family. When she gets a bonus, he gets touchy and orders
her to give it back. This is a good example of how people act
under pressure. When we are sick, poor, hopeless, and
distressed, we forget all the virtues we practiced, and often
we take it out on others. It's almost as if this world with its
problems was created just so we could learn who we are.

Tobit 2:9–14
Psalm 112:1–2,7–8,9
Mark 12:13–17

*Jesus said to them, "Are you not misled
because you do not know the scriptures
or the power of God?"*
—MARK 12:24

Nowadays it is easy to be misled by the posts and articles in
social media. If, by reading the Scriptures and praying, we
know the power of God to create, to lead, to heal, to
provide, to forgive, and to save, then it is protection against
misleading stuff from other people. It is not foolproof, but it
will certainly help.

Tobit 3:1–11a,16–17a
Psalm 25:2–3,4–5ab,6 and 7bc,8–9
Mark 12:18–27

Thursday

JUNE 3

• ST. CHARLES LWANGA AND COMPANIONS, MARTYRS •

Tobiah arose from bed and said to his wife,
"My love, get up.
Let us pray and beg our Lord to have mercy on us
and to grant us deliverance."
She got up, and they started to pray
and beg that deliverance might be theirs.
—TOBIT 8:4B–5A

What these two praying lovebirds don't realize is that the angel Raphael has already taken care of the demon who had killed Sarah's seven previous husbands. He used a stinky fish to chase the demon away. If you haven't read the book of Tobit, I recommend it. It has everything: afflictions, social humiliations, worried parents, travel adventures, an angel, a demon, and two star-crossed lovers. Someone should make it into a movie.

Tobit 6:10–11; 7:1bcde,9–17; 8:4–9a
Psalm 128:1–2,3,4–5
Mark 12:28–34

"Blessed be God,
and praised be his great name,
and blessed be all his holy angels.
May his holy name be praised
throughout all the ages,
Because it was he who scourged me,
and it is he who has had mercy on me."

—TOBIT 11:14–15A

The "scourge" that Tobit is referring to is the blindness he contracted after sleeping under a bird roost where the droppings fell into his eyes, causing cataracts. I'm not sure why he says that God caused this scourge. Sometimes we blame God for accidents and natural disasters. When Tobit receives his sight back from the application of fish gall to his cataracts, he blames the cure on God as well. At least Tobit is evenhanded about the blame and the credit.

Tobit 11:5–17
Psalm 146:1b–2,6c–7,8–9a,9bc–10
Mark 12:35–37

Saturday

JUNE 5

• ST. BONIFACE, BISHOP AND MARTYR •

Raphael called the two men aside privately
and said to them:
"Thank God! Give him the praise and the glory.
Before all the living,
acknowledge the many good things
he has done for you,
by blessing and extolling his name in song.
Honor and proclaim God's deeds,
and do not be slack in praising him.
A king's secret it is prudent to keep,
but the works of God are to be declared
and made known."
—TOBIT 12:6B,7

I do not give God the glory nearly enough. Any good I have done comes from God. Any bravery I have shown is the Lord's strength within me. Every time I am healed, every bite of food I take, and the bed I sleep in are all gifts from our good God. These very words on this page are written only after prayer. It's all God. I praise him!

Tobit 12:1,5–15,20
Tobit 13:2,6efgh,7,8
Mark 12:38–44

Sunday

JUNE 6

• THE MOST HOLY BODY AND BLOOD OF CHRIST (CORPUS CHRISTI) •

While they were eating,
he took bread, said the blessing,
broke it, gave it to them, and said,
"Take it; this is my body."
—MARK 14:22

Jesus wants so badly to live in us that he gave this sacrament by which we actually eat of his body and drink his blood. For most of my life I missed the point. I received the holy bread and wine, prayed gratefully, and hoped that it worked: that I would become holy. It has occurred to me only in recent years that Jesus wants to *live inside me*. Jesus wants to fill me up with his love, his strength, and his mercy. He wants me to forget about doing anything by myself. He is telling us that we are capable of holding him inside ourselves. We only need to invite him in.

Exodus 24:3–8
Psalm 116:12–13,15–16,17–18(13)
Hebrews 9:11–15
Mark 14:12–16,22–26

Monday
JUNE 7

"Blessed are the clean of heart
for they will see God."
—MATTHEW 5:8

This is my favorite beatitude because I want to see God, and
Jesus tells us how that happens. We need only have a clean
heart, and we will see God. This is true. My heart is clean on
those rare occasions when I listen well to someone, without
judging, without impatience, and without envy. When I
release the impurities from my ego and look with love and
compassion on another person, I can see God in them. I can
see love, mercy, kindness—whatever bit of God they hold. It
is a glorious sight to see God in another person, and I am
truly blessed in those moments.

2 Corinthians 1:1–7
Psalm 34:2–3,4–5,6–7,8–9
Matthew 5:1–12

Jesus said to his disciples:
"You are the salt of the earth.
But if salt loses its taste, with what can it be seasoned?
It is no longer good for anything
but to be thrown out and trampled underfoot."
—MATTHEW 5:13

Jesus is talking nonsense here. Salt is an element—it can't
lose its taste. It is what it is. But because we know that Jesus
doesn't talk nonsense, let's look at his words again. If we are
salt, then we are an element, part of what the universe is
made of. We are not a by-product of creation, nor are we a
combination of things that can be put together in different
ways. I think he is speaking of our souls, not our bodies. Our
souls are part of what makes up the universe. Our souls are an
essential element in creation—like salt.

2 Corinthians 1:18–22
Psalm 119:129,130,131,132,133,135
Matthew 5:13–16

Wednesday

JUNE 9

For if what was going to fade was glorious,
how much more will what endures be glorious.
—2 CORINTHIANS 3:11

Many saints and spiritual writers have recommended the observation of nature. Jesus said, "Consider the flowers . . ." and Saint Francis of Assisi composed songs about the sun and moon and all of nature. In 2 Corinthians, Paul is writing about the fading of the law of Moses and how the law of love and righteousness will supersede it. He doesn't discount the glory of God's Ten Commandments; rather, he insists that Jesus has given us *more glory*. Today, find a flower, or a plant, or a cat, or a bird, and contemplate it for ten minutes. Then remind yourself that your soul is eternal. It is so much more glorious than the flower or cat. God made your soul. God loves your soul.

2 Corinthians 3:4–11
Psalm 99:5,6,7,8,9
Matthew 5:17–19

⇒ 193 ⇐

Thursday

JUNE 10

Therefore, if you bring your gift to the altar,
and there recall that your brother
has anything against you,
leave your gift there at the altar,
go first and be reconciled with your brother, and then come and offer
your gift.
—MATTHEW 5:23–24

This is excellent advice. It's like the advice given to married couples: *never go to bed angry*. I've been married thirty-six years, and I admit that I have gone to bed disgruntled a few times. I have also gone to Mass on Sunday fuming over something that happened earlier in the week between me and a friend or colleague. This verse from Matthew comes to my mind, but wanting to reconcile instantly isn't always in the cards. I'm getting better at it. My goal is to make my love, not my grudges, eternal.

2 Corinthians 3:15—4:1,3–6
Psalm 85:9ab and 10,11–12,13–14
Matthew 5:20–26

⇒ 194 ⇐

Friday

JUNE 11

• THE SACRED HEART OF JESUS •

I fostered them like one
who raises an infant to his cheeks;
Yet, though I stooped to feed my child,
they did not know that I was their healer.
—HOSEA 11:3C,4B,C

For many years I have puzzled over the image of the Sacred
Heart of Jesus. In paintings, his heart is sitting outside his
body on his chest, typically pierced and bleeding. One hand
points to his heart, and his mild gaze is fixed straight ahead
at the viewer. He does not appear to be suffering but looks
more like a teacher trying hard to convey something to
obtuse students. I am one of those. Although I can't
remember ever reading it before, I like this quote from
Hosea. Jesus is every kind of love here: he cuddles, he stoops
down, he feeds, and he heals. This helps me understand the
Sacred Heart a tiny bit.

Hosea 11:1,3–4,8c–9
Isaiah 12:2–3,4,5–6(3)
Ephesians 3:8–12,14–19
John 19:31–37

When his parents saw him
they were astonished,
and his mother said to him,
"Son, why have you done this to us?
Your father and I have been looking for you
with great anxiety."
—LUKE 2:48

Perhaps Mary looks for all her children with great anxiety. If she hadn't found Jesus in three days' time, you can bet that she would have kept looking for as long as it took. Mary feels this way about each of us. She will not give up, so we may as well stop avoiding her. Turn your thoughts to Mary today. She keeps you in her heart.

2 Corinthians 5:14–21
Psalm 103:1–2,3–4,9–10,11–12
Luke 2:41–51

*Without parables he did not speak to them,
but to his own disciples he explained everything
in private.*

—MARK 4:34

I think my entire life is a parable. Every person who walks
into it, every crisis, every joy, all that surrounds me—it is all
part of God's story. And it all has meaning. Jesus is speaking
softly to me through the people and circumstances in my life.
But, like his disciples, I need to sit still with him, listening in
the privacy of my prayer space, in order to understand my
parable life.

Ezekiel 17:22–24
Psalm 92:2–3,13–14,15–16
2 Corinthians 5:6–10
Mark 4:26–34

Jesus said to his disciples:
"You have heard it was said,
An eye for an eye and a tooth for a tooth.
But I say to you, offer no resistance to one who is evil.
When someone strikes you on your right cheek,
turn the other one to him as well.
If anyone wants to go to law with you over your tunic,
hand him your cloak as well."
—MATTHEW 5:38–40

Make no mistake: Jesus ordered us to be nonviolent. Through his trial, brutal beating, and crucifixion, he showed us how. Then he said, "Follow me." It was St. Augustine, not Jesus, who wrote about a *just war*, and people prefer to follow that philosophy because Jesus' way requires humility. His is the narrow way that leads to life. War leads to death: *he who lives by the sword, dies by the sword.*

2 Corinthians 6:1–10
Psalm 98:1,2b,3ab,3cd–4
Matthew 5:38–42

Tuesday

JUNE 15

We want you to know, brothers and sisters,
of the grace of God
that has been given to the churches of Macedonia,
for in a severe test of affliction,
the abundance of their joy and their profound poverty
overflowed in a wealth of generosity on their part.
—2 CORINTHIANS 8:1–2

These Macedonians are like the people we help at St. Vincent de Paul. One man who needed our assistance told me, "I pray each day that no matter how tight the money is, I will always have something to put in the plate at church. Last Sunday I was walking up the church steps without a penny in my pocket and I felt terrible. A fellow was coming out the door, and he paused, pressed a five into my palm, and said, 'It's a good day to be blessed, brother.' God answered my prayer!"

2 Corinthians 8:1–9
Psalm 146:2,5–6ab,6c–7,8–9a
Matthew 5:43–48

Wednesday

JUNE 16

Each must do as already determined,
without sadness or compulsion,
for God loves a cheerful giver.
—2 CORINTHIANS 9:7

If being a cheerful giver is an easy way to make God happy,
whyever would we not do it? Giving is not so hard, but
giving cheerfully requires more of us. I try to smile joyfully at
the usher who extends the offering basket across the pew
toward me. If you watch, you'll see that ushers don't get a lot
of smiles. It is also better to beam at panhandlers when
handing them a little money. On a day when I apologized
because I didn't have cash, a shabbily dressed man said to me,
"Just keep smiling, dear. It's okay." I'm certain he was Jesus in
disguise.

2 Corinthians 9:6–11
Psalm 112:1bc–2,3–4,9
Matthew 6:1–6,16–18

⇒200⇐

JUNE 17

"This is how you are to pray:
Our Father who art in heaven,
hallowed be thy name,
thy Kingdom come,
thy will be done,
on earth as it is in heaven.
Give us this day our daily bread;
and forgive us our trespasses,
as we forgive those who trespass against us;
and lead us not into temptation,
but deliver us from evil."
—MATTHEW 6:9–10

Jesus says a strong prayer here. I can almost hear him saying, "First—no sniveling or whining." He listens to our prayers, so it's understandable that he doesn't want us saying things like "If only you would help me, I promise I'll never sin again." Or "No one is being fair to me, God!" Jesus knew that fathers don't tolerate whining.

2 Corinthians 11:1–11
Psalm 111:1b–2,3–4,7–8
Matthew 6:7–15

JUNE 18

Jesus said to his disciples:
"Do not store up for yourselves treasures on earth,
where moth and decay destroy, and thieves
break in and steal.
But store up treasures in heaven,
where neither moth nor decay destroys,
nor thieves break in and steal.
For where your treasure is, there also will your heart be."
—MATTHEW 6:19–21

We all know that we mustn't cling to the things we own, that letting go of possessions, power, money, reputations, even our expertise and opinions, is the only way to be truly free. Jesus is holding out to us the freedom of being nobody: the freedom of being a little child again. It takes a lifetime to make that kind of treasure our heart's desire.

2 Corinthians 11:18,21–30
Psalm 34:2–3,4–5,6–7
Matthew 6:19–23

*"Do not worry about tomorrow; tomorrow
will take care of itself.
Sufficient for a day is its own evil."*
—MATTHEW 6:34

We are not given the option of knowing the future. God
created us to live one day at a time. If we could know the
future, then we would either make plans accordingly or
despair completely. But Jesus is telling us that we were not
created that way. *We cannot know the future because it is not set in
stone; we help create it with our every word and action.* Concentrate
on today: do your work, take care of the people around you,
love yourself and everyone else, tend the earth, and thank
God. The future will take care of itself.

2 Corinthians 12:1–10
Psalm 34:8–9,10–11,12–13
Matthew 6:24–34

Sunday

JUNE 20

• TWELFTH SUNDAY IN ORDINARY TIME •

Then he asked them, "Why are you terrified?
Do you not yet have faith?"
—MARK 4:40

Fear, then, is the opposite of faith.

Job 38:1,8–11
Psalm 107:23–24,25–26,28–29,30–31(1b)
2 Corinthians 5:14–17
Mark 4:35–41

Monday

JUNE 21

• ST. ALOYSIUS GONZAGA, RELIGIOUS •

*"How can you say to your brother,
'Let me remove that splinter from your eye,'
while the wooden beam is in your eye?
You hypocrite, remove the wooden beam
from your eye first;
then you will see clearly
to remove the splinter from your brother's eye."*
—MATTHEW 7:4–5

If you don't cringe at this verse, then you don't need to read any further today. You're fine: you are not a judgmental person. I am. I judge people for the way they drive, the way they cut in line, the way they eat, how they vote, how they litter, and how much they drink. I condemn people for condemning others. If someone doesn't like me, I think there must be something wrong with that person. There is a huge log in my eye, but I am working on getting it out. I ask for your patience for the remainder of this book.

Genesis 12:1–9
Psalm 33:12–13,18–19,20 and 22
Matthew 7:1–5

Tuesday

JUNE 22

• ST. PAULINUS OF NOLA, BISHOP • ST. JOHN FISHER, BISHOP, AND
ST. THOMAS MORE, MARTYRS •

> *"Do to others whatever you would have them do to you.*
> *This is the Law and Prophets."*
> —MATTHEW 7:12

Extroverts read this and bring casseroles, pick up the phone,
throw surprise parties, and give big hugs. Introverts read this
same passage and sit in silence with the grieving, send texts,
wrap up pretty packages, and beam at people.

Genesis 13:2,5–18
Psalm 15:2–3a,3bc–4ab,5
Matthew 7:6,12–14

Wednesday

JUNE 23

"Beware of false prophets, who come to you
in sheep's clothing,
but underneath are ravenous wolves.
By their fruits you will know them."
—MATTHEW 7:15–16A

I look at Jesus' warning and sigh. How is it that we didn't recognize the ravenous wolves who preyed on children when the wolves were disguised as priests, bishops, and other church authorities? And when some innocent did point them out, why did we believe the ones wearing sheep's clothing and not the children? Jesus knows we are easily fooled by appearances.

Genesis 15:1–12,17–18
Psalm 105:1–2,3–4,6–7,8–9
Matthew 7:15–20

Thursday

JUNE 24

• THE NATIVITY OF ST. JOHN THE BAPTIST •

John heralded his coming by proclaiming a baptism
of repentance
to all the people of Israel;
and as John was completing his course, he would say,
"What do you suppose that I am? I am not he.
Behold, one is coming after me;
I am not worthy to unfasten the sandals of his feet."
—ACTS 13:24–25

John is both bold and humble—two qualities not generally found in the same person. Do you know someone like him? Think about boldness and humility, and ponder everyone you can think of. It seems to me that these are the prime attributes of sainthood, along with deep, abiding love. Perhaps you know a saint.

VIGIL:
Jeremiah 1:4–10
Psalm 71:1–2,3–4a,5–6ab,15ab and 17
1 Peter 1:8–12
Luke 1:5–17

DAY:
Isaiah 49:1–6
Psalm 139:1b–3,13–14ab,14c–15
Acts 13:22–26
Luke 1:57–66,80

Friday

JUNE 25

When Abram was ninety-nine years old,
the LORD appeared to him
and said: "I am God the Almighty.
Walk in my presence and be blameless."
—GENESIS 17:1

Probably, every ninety-nine-year-old gets this same invitation. The rest of what God says to Abram is not the usual spiritual program: the circumcision, the multigenerational covenant, the new baby, etc. But this bit about being invited to walk in God's presence—that's the end game for all of us. That is where we are all going. So, be ready. If God appears and tells you to stop sinning and walk close to him, that is not an illusion. Listen up.

Genesis 17:1,9–10,15–22
Psalm 128:1–2,3,4–5
Matthew 8:1–4

Saturday

JUNE 26

When Jesus entered Capernaum,
a centurion approached him and appealed
to him, saying,
"Lord, my servant is lying at home paralyzed,
suffering dreadfully."
He said to him, "I will come and cure him."
The centurion said in reply,
"Lord, I am not worthy to have you enter
under my roof;
only say the word and my servant will be healed."
—MATTHEW 8:5–8

In the Roman Catholic Mass, we all quote the centurion before we receive communion. The centurion: a pagan member of the occupying army. Observant Jews of the time would have been made ritually impure by going into his home, but Jesus doesn't hesitate to offer to come. I love this story. I love that we say this during every Mass. At our invitation, Jesus will most certainly come and heal us no matter who we are.

Genesis 18:1–15
Luke 1:46–47,48–49,50 and 53,54–55
Matthew 8:5–17

Sunday

JUNE 27

She had heard about Jesus and came up behind him
in the crowd
and touched his cloak.
She said, "If I but touch his clothes, I shall be cured."
—MARK 5:27–28

The crowd is pressing around Jesus. He is probably hard to distinguish in the hubbub and noise. A leader of the people has requested his help, and they are on their way to the man's sick daughter. Everyone is excited about what might happen, because Jesus, by this time, has a reputation as a healer. This woman knows that she is unclean because of her issue of blood: she shouldn't even be here. Yet she wiggles through the moving crowd and reaches out as far as she can, hoping to touch Jesus' garments. That's all she wants, just to reach up and touch him. This is a wonderful picture of prayer.

Wisdom 1:13–15; 2:23–24
Psalm 30:2,4,5–6,11,12,13(2a)
2 Corinthians 8:7,9,13–15
Mark 5:21–43 or 5:21–24,35b–43

Monday

JUNE 28

• ST. IRENAEUS, BISHOP AND MARTYR •

A scribe approached and said to him,
"Teacher, I will follow you wherever you go."
Jesus answered him, "Foxes have dens and birds
of the sky have nests,
but the Son of Man has nowhere to rest his head."
Another of his disciples said to him,
"Lord, let me go first and bury my father."
But Jesus answered him "Follow me,
and let the dead bury their dead."
—MATTHEW 8:19–22

Here's that message again: *Let go of everything.* Let go of home, of a bed to sleep in, of family, and of ancestors. When I cling to earthly security, either physical or emotional, I do not cling to God. And then God has a difficult time using me for his purpose of loving everyone and everything.

Genesis 18:16–33
Psalm 103:1b–2,3–4,8–9,10–11
Matthew 8:18–22

Tuesday

JUNE 29

• ST. PETER AND ST. PAUL, APOSTLES •

The Lord will rescue me from every evil threat
and will bring me safe to his heavenly Kingdom.
To him be glory forever and ever. Amen.
—2 TIMOTHY 4:17–18

I once visited a church named St. Peter in Chains. Paul is writing this letter from prison while wearing chains, yet he affirms in the strongest language that God will rescue him from evil and bring him to heaven. This is our faith. There will certainly be trials, but we will always be with God. And at the end of our days, God will rescue us from our chains so that we can live with him forever. From his prison cell, Paul could see this earth plainly (read the rest of this letter). He could also see beyond it. Today, look out from your prison and see God waiting to meet you.

<table>
<tr><td>VIGIL:</td><td>DAY:</td></tr>
<tr><td>Acts 3:1–10</td><td>Acts 12:1–11</td></tr>
<tr><td>Psalm 19:2–3,4–5</td><td>Psalm 34:2–3,4–5,6–7,8–9</td></tr>
<tr><td>Galatians 1:11–20</td><td>2 Timothy 4:6–8,17–18</td></tr>
<tr><td>John 21:15–19</td><td>Matthew 16:13–19</td></tr>
</table>

JUNE 30

• THE FIRST MARTYRS OF THE HOLY ROMAN CHURCH •

The Lord hears the cry of the poor.
—PSALM 34:7A

The poor have many reasons to cry out to the Lord for help:
hunger, homelessness, no heat, no insurance, and no
transportation. But in my experience, after years of praying
with people in distressing economic situations, the poor cry
out most often in thanksgiving. So many times, when the
St. Vincent de Paul members tell them that their bill will be
paid, our dear friends in need exclaim, "Thank you, Jesus!" or
"God is good!" or "Alleluia!" To me, it is no surprise that God
hears the cry of the poor.

Genesis 21:5,8–20a
Psalm 34:7–8,10–11,12–13
Matthew 8:28–34

Thursday

JULY 1

• ST. JUNÍPERO SERRA, PRIEST •

*"Which is easier, to say, 'Your sins are forgiven,'
or to say, 'Rise and walk'?"*
—MATTHEW 9:5

Which is easier, to say, "I forgive you," or to say, "Will you forgive me?" Either way, say it. Then rise and walk.

Genesis 22:1b–19
Psalm 115:1–2,3–4,5–6,8–9
Matthew 9:1–8

Friday
JULY 2

"Go and learn the meaning of the words,
I desire mercy, not sacrifice.
I did not come to call the righteous but sinners."
—MATTHEW 9:13

What is God's will? What is God's will for my life? What is God's will for my family? What is God's will for our church? What is God's will for our country? What is God's will for the world? Go and learn the meaning of the words *I desire mercy, not sacrifice.* Mercy is God's will. Stop sacrificing yourself and family, stop sacrificing the church, stop sacrificing the entire country and the entire world. God wants mercy, not sacrifice.

Be merciful to yourself, forgive your parents and your children, be forgiving of the church, let the past sins of the politicians and the world leaders go. Let it all go for God's sake. Go and learn how to be merciful as God is merciful.

Genesis 23:1–4,19; 24:1–8,62–67
Psalm 106:1b–2,3–4a,4b–5
Matthew 9:9–13

Saturday

JULY 3

• ST. THOMAS, APOSTLE •

Then he said to Thomas, "Put your finger here and
see my hands,
and bring your hand and put it into my side,
and do not be unbelieving, but believe."
—JOHN 20:27

Thomas's story is about not hanging on to incredulity.
Believe. Just believe. After a particularly moving religious
service, the friend who was sitting at my side said to me,
"Jane, wasn't that amazing to see the angel standing behind
Fr. Mike?" I stared at her and said, "The angel?" She was
shocked. "You didn't see him? He was huge! Are you sure you
didn't see him? Were you looking another way? He was
standing right there!"

I choose to believe her, and it brings me great joy. After all,
what will incredulity bring me? Nothing, absolutely nothing.
Believe. Just believe. Joy waits for you.

Ephesians 2:19–22
Psalm 117:1bc,2
John 20:24–29

Three times I begged the Lord about this,
that it might leave me,
but he said to me, "My grace is sufficient for you,
for power is made perfect in weakness."
I will rather boast most gladly of my weaknesses,
in order that the power of Christ may dwell with me.
—2 CORINTHIANS 12:8–9

Where is your weakness? It is important to answer this question because God's power dwells in our weakness, not in our strength. Are you good at organization? Then that is your power. So what? It is a measly human power. Is it difficult for you to meet new people? That is your weakness, and you can be sure that God will work through that flaw to bring about his kingdom. God's power is in your weakness. So meditate, ask God, and find your weakness. Then be glad like Paul.

Ezekiel 2:2–5
Psalm 123:1–2,2,3–4
2 Corinthians 12:7–10
Mark 6:1–6

• ST. ELIZABETH OF PORTUGAL • ST. ANTHONY MARY ZACCARIA, PRIEST •

For he will rescue you from the snare of the fowler,
from the destroying pestilence.
With his pinions he will cover you,
and under his wings you shall take refuge.
—PSALM 91:3–4A

When my daughter lived in Japan, she asked her Japanese
friend why they put dragons on their headstones. He
explained that the dragons were there to protect the dead in
the next life. He asked her about Christian images on graves,
and she told him we put doves and lambs on the headstones.
He was astounded that we would put trust in meek creatures
to guard us in the next life. This conversation opened my
eyes to my own faith: I *do* trust in the meekness of Jesus. God
covers us with "his pinions," not with his teeth.

Genesis 28:10–22a
Psalm 91:1–2,3–4,14–15ab
Matthew 9:18–26

JULY 6

• ST. MARIA GORETTI, VIRGIN AND MARTYR •

At sunrise, as he left Penuel,
Jacob limped along because of his hip.
—GENESIS 32:32

Jacob is one of my favorite characters in the Bible. His personal honesty is not consistent, and his family problems rival those of any family that ever lived on earth. Yet he sincerely believes in God. God visits him from time to time, and those encounters are entertaining and otherworldly. This particular story finds Jacob wrestling with the divine. In the end, he doesn't lose, and he receives a new name and a dislocated hip. His new name is Israel, and now he limps. When you struggle with the divine, do you ever feel that your self-understanding changes? And is your way of walking not so strong? Not so even? Not so sure of yourself? That's how it is for me, too.

Genesis 32:23–33
Psalm 17:1b,2–3,6–7ab,8b and 15
Matthew 9:32–38

Wednesday

July 7

When the famine had spread throughout the land,
Joseph opened all the cities that had grain
and rationed it to the Egyptians,
since the famine had gripped the land of Egypt.
In fact, all the world came to Joseph to obtain
rations of grain,
for famine had gripped the whole world.
—GENESIS 41:56–57

The Egyptians, led by Pharaoh's dream and Joseph's practical hoarding, were prepared to weather the famine that gripped the world. Did they defend their hoard and protect their borders against the hungry people coming from other countries? No, apparently not. They must have understood that we are all connected. Our neighbor's survival is our survival.

Genesis 41:55–57; 42:5–7a,17–24a
Psalm 33:2–3,10–11,18–19
Matthew 10:1–7

Thursday

JULY 8

When the Lord called down a famine on the land
and ruined the crop that sustained them,
He sent a man before them,
Joseph, sold as a slave.
—PSALM 105:16–17

When the famine struck, the person who had the wisdom to help the Egyptian people survive was not one of them. Joseph was a foreigner, a person sold as a slave and then falsely accused and imprisoned. Pharaoh called him out of prison to interpret his dream, then appointed him to lead them through the predicted crisis. Such love God sends in the disguise of the most wretched person among us! Look closely at the next panhandler you meet. Pray to God that you may recognize your salvation.

Genesis 44:18–21,23b–29; 45:1–5
Psalm 105:16–17,18–19,20–21
Matthew 10:7–15

Friday

JULY 9

• ST. AUGUSTINE ZHAO RONG, PRIEST, AND COMPANIONS, MARTYRS •

There God, speaking to Israel in a vision by night called:
"Jacob! Jacob!"
He answered, "Here I am."
Then he said: "I am God, the God of your father.
Do not be afraid to go down to Egypt,
for there I will make you a great nation.
Not only will I go down to Egypt with you;
I will also bring you back here, after Joseph
has closed your eyes." . . .

Thus Jacob and all his descendants migrated to Egypt.
His sons and his grandsons, his daughters
and his granddaughters—
all his descendants—he took with him to Egypt.
—GENESIS 46:2–4,6B–7

Because of the famine, Jacob migrated, but he also was afraid.
God sent him, and God stayed with him. It seems that
battling the migration of hungry, desperate people can lead
us into battling God himself.

Genesis 46:1–7,28–30
Psalm 37:3–4,18–19,27–28,39–40
Matthew 10:16–23

*"And do not be afraid of those who kill the body but
cannot kill the soul;
rather, be afraid of the one who can destroy
both soul and body in Gehenna."*
—MATTHEW 10:28

In the nine verses of Matthew today, Jesus tells his disciples
three times, "Do not be afraid." *Do not be afraid* is one of his
most basic commandments, so it is not surprising to see it
repeated. However, in verse 28, he turns it around and tells
them to be afraid of losing their souls and bodies in hell.
Okay, then fear can protect us in this instance? Do not be
afraid of other people's evil but be afraid of our own. Do not
fear the sin of persecution and murder against us, but be very
afraid of the sins of pride, judgment, and hate within
us—very, very afraid.

Genesis 49:29–32; 50:15–26a
Psalm 105:1–2,3–4,6–7
Matthew 10:24–33

*Jesus summoned the Twelve and began to send them out
two by two
and gave them authority over unclean spirits.*
—MARK 6:7

Today let's look at how Jesus sends out his apostles. First: He summoned them. This wasn't a mission they requested. They were not, apparently, eager to launch into the work by themselves. Second: He sent them in pairs. Two persons is a small, unthreatening group. Third: They did not pick and choose what they wanted to do or where they wanted to go—*they were sent.* Fourth: He gave them authority over unclean spirits. He did not give them authority to condemn or punish people. He did not give them authority to form exclusive groups. He did not give them authority to collect buildings, land, or precious objects.

Amos 7:12–15
Psalm 85:9–10,11–12,13–14(8)
Ephesians 1:3–14 or 1:3–10
Mark 6:7–13

Monday

JULY 12

Jesus said to his Apostles: . . .
"For I have come to set
a man against his father,
a daughter against her mother,
and a daughter-in-law against her mother-in-law;
and one's enemies will be those of his household."
—MATTHEW 10:35–36

This means that clannishness is not part of following Jesus. He must have known how we love to identify our ancestry and share it proudly. When vacationing in Ireland, in the town where my great-grandfather came from, we found the grave site of the family. They were mostly Patricks and Catherines, like many of the family in the United States. When a local cousin asked my name and I answered, "Jane," he frowned and said, "That's too bad." I had never thought about how my first name came from the English side of the family and how unfortunate the Irish side would view it. Jesus rejected clannishness for good reason.

Exodus 1:8–14,22
Psalm 124:1b–3,4–6,7–8
Matthew 10:34—11:1

Tuesday

JULY 13

• ST. HENRY •

Pharaoh's daughter came down to the river to bathe,
while her maids walked along the river bank.
Noticing the basket among the reeds,
she sent her handmaid to fetch it.
On opening it, she looked, and lo,
there was a baby boy, crying!
She was moved with pity for him and said,
"It is one of the Hebrews' children."
—EXODUS 1:5–6

Pharaoh had ordered that all the newborn baby boys of the Hebrews be killed. Yet here is his daughter saving one of them. People are complicated. This is a good reminder not to judge people because of their family, their institutions, or their government.

Exodus 2:1–15a
Psalm 69:3,14,30–31,33–34
Matthew 11:20–24

≥227≤

Wednesday
JULY 14

• ST. KATERI TEKAKWITHA, VIRGIN •

At that time Jesus exclaimed:
"I give praise to you, Father, Lord of heaven and earth,
for although you have hidden these things
from the wise and the learned
you have revealed them to the childlike."
—MATTHEW 11:25

It is fine to be naive. It is also fine not to worry about things outside my control. Spending an hour sitting in the grass and watching ants is not a waste of time. Taking a nap when I am tired is not laziness. Running up to people when I am super happy to see them is only love. Listening to stories and looking at pictures is a fun way to learn about the world. And not feeling entirely independent is also childlike grace. To believe that everything we think and do is obvious and known to our parents is how children think. Might this be how God reveals himself to the childlike?

Exodus 3:1–6,9–12
Psalm 103:1b–2,3–4,6–7
Matthew 11:25–27

God replied, "I am who am."
—EXODUS 3:14A

This is God's answer to Moses' question of *who are you?* God is using the verb *to be* conjugated in the present tense, as I *am;* you (singular) *are;* he, she, it *is;* we *are;* you (plural) *are;* they *are.* What does this tell me? First: God exists. *To be* means to exist. Second: God is first-person singular; there is only one God. Third: God is in the present tense; God is here, now. The fundamentals about God are wrapped up in this one little statement.

Exodus 3:13–20
Psalm 105:1 and 5,8–9,24–25,26–27
Matthew 11:28–30

Friday

JULY 16

• OUR LADY OF MOUNT CARMEL •

"This is how you are to eat it:
with your loins girt, sandals on your feet
and your staff in hand,
you shall eat like those who are in flight.
It is the Passover of the LORD."
—EXODUS 11:11

At this awe-inspiring moment when the Lord is about to lead
his people out of slavery to the Promised Land, he instructs
them to eat their last meal dressed for flight. If I want God to
lead me, is it necessary for me to dress for flight? Should I
prepare to leave everything from my old life behind? Should
I be ready to go at a moment's notice?

Exodus 11:10—12:14
Psalm 116:12–13,15 and 16bc,17–18
Matthew 12:1–8

⇒ 230 ⇐

The time the children of Israel had stayed in Egypt
was four hundred and thirty years.
At the end of four hundred and thirty years,
all the hosts of the LORD left the land of Egypt
on this very date.
—EXODUS 12:40–41

Four hundred thirty years ago was around AD 1600. At that time, Spain ruled the current states of California, Nevada, Colorado, Utah, New Mexico, Arizona, Texas, Oregon, Washington, Florida, and parts of Idaho, Montana, Wyoming, Kansas, Oklahoma, and Louisiana, as well as what is now Mexico, part of British Columbia, Guatemala, Costa Rica, El Salvador, Honduras, Nicaragua, Cuba, Dominican Republic, Puerto Rico, and Trinidad. This territory was all called New Spain. Borders, governments, and populations can change a lot in 430 years. Picture yourself about to leave your home of 430 years on God's order. What do you fear? What is your hope? Will you grumble?

Exodus 12:37–42
Psalm 136:1 and 23–24,10–12,13–15
Matthew 12:14–21

Sunday

JULY 18

• SIXTEENTH SUNDAY IN ORDINARY TIME •

He came and preached peace to you who were far off
and peace to those who were near,
for through him we both have access in one Spirit
to the Father.
—EPHESIANS 2:17–18

Both we who are far off and we who are near have access in
the Spirit to the Father through Jesus. All have access to
God. We do not have to wait outside, hoping that God will
hear someone else's prayer for us. It is not necessary that we
are born into the "right" family, clan, religion, or nationality.
We can whisper the name *Jesus* with mixed motives and a
sin-filled past, and God will hear. What keeps us from doing
this? Our ego says, *You don't believe all that nonsense; you can*
manage without God; you will feel like a fool if you let him come in;
God doesn't care about you. Our ego does not "preach peace."

Jeremiah 23:1–6
Psalm 23:1–3,3–4,5,6(1)
Ephesians 2:13–18
Mark 6:30–34

*"The LORD himself will fight for you; you have
only to keep still."*
—EXODUS 14:14

Our culture tells us to "keep busy," but God keeps telling us
to "keep still." A friend asked me to pray that she "will keep
busy." That would be a contradictory prayer. I couldn't do it.

Tuesday

JULY 20

• ST. APOLLINARIUS, BISHOP AND MARTYR •

"Who is my mother? Who are my brothers?"
And stretching out his hand toward his disciples, he said,
"Here are my mother and my brothers.
For whoever does the will of my heavenly Father
is my brother, and sister, and mother."
—MATTHEW 12:48B–50

I think that sometimes the churchy/biblical language we use is so well-worn that we don't hear the message any longer. I ask your patience and your imagination for a moment while I render Jesus' statement in slightly different words. It is not that I want to change the meaning—quite the opposite: I want the meaning to jump out. Here goes:

"Who is my family?" And pointing at the people reading, he said, "You are part of my family, and I am part of your family. For you are seeking God's voice and loving those you meet each day, which is what God our father asks of us."

Exodus 14:21—15:1
Exodus 15:8–9,10 and 12,17
Matthew 12:46–50

• ST. LAWRENCE OF BRINDISI, PRIEST AND DOCTOR OF THE CHURCH •

Then Moses said to Aaron, "Tell the whole congregation
of the children of Israel:
Present yourselves before the LORD,
for he has heard your grumbling."
When Aaron announced this to the whole
assembly of the children of Israel,
they turned toward the desert, and lo,
the glory of the LORD appeared in the cloud!
—EXODUS 16:9–10

Aaron tells the grumbling Israelites to present themselves
before the Lord . . . so they turn toward the desert. Doesn't
this strike you as odd? Wouldn't you look toward the
mountains? Or place yourself before a holy altar to pray? Or
gather together and intone songs? Perhaps I do not know
how to present myself before the Lord. I need to think about
where the desert is in my life and turn toward that so I am
standing before the Lord with my grumbles. In the desert I
will see his glory.

Exodus 16:1–5,9–15
Psalm 78:18–19,23–24,25–26,27–28
Matthew 13:1–9

So she ran and went to Simon Peter and to the other disciple whom Jesus loved, and told them, "They have taken the Lord from the tomb, and we don't know where they put him."

—JOHN 20:2

Mary didn't know where to find Jesus. Sometimes, we don't know where to find him either. We expect him to be in one place, but it turns out he's in another. It would be nice if Jesus gave us his itinerary, but faith doesn't work that way. We always must do some searching. It exercises our desire, our wisdom, and our love.

Song of Songs 3:1–4b or 2 Corinthians 5:14–17
Psalm 63:2,3–4,5–6,8–9
John 20:1–2,11–18

Friday

JULY 23

• ST. BRIDGET OF SWEDEN, RELIGIOUS •

"You shall not covet your neighbor's house.
You shall not covet your neighbor's wife,
nor his male or female slave, nor his ox or ass,
nor anything else that belongs to him."
—EXODUS 20:17

The Ten Commandments are the precepts of the Lord that the psalmists all praise joyfully. Plenty of attention is given to the first three about honoring God. Number four is about honoring our parents. Then we have the prohibitory ones: no killing, no adultery, no stealing, and no false witnessing. The last two are the ones that take place in our heads: no coveting what belongs to our neighbor. It must be that our thoughts are powerful. Someone once told me that "all thoughts are either prayers or curses." Coveting is the sin of desiring someone else's blessings. We should, instead, desire blessing for our neighbors—which is prayer.

Exodus 20:1–17
Psalm 19:8,9,10,11
Matthew 13:18–23

*"Offer to God praise as your sacrifice
and fulfill your vows to the Most High;"*
—PSALM 50:14

We believe that God is almighty, creator, omniscient, humble, and good, among other things. Obviously, with these characteristics, God does not need our human praises. If he does need to hear us exult him and tell him how wonderful he is—that would mean that he is neither humble nor wise, nor almighty, nor even very good. It must be that *we* need to praise God. That makes sense because we are the ones who need to be reminded that we are not almighty, not omniscient, not humble, not always good, and we certainly did not create the earth. Praising God is a simple way to remember that we are not God.

Exodus 24:3–8
Psalm 50:1b–2,5–6,14–15
Matthew 13:24–30

Sunday

JULY 25

• SEVENTEENTH SUNDAY IN ORDINARY TIME •

The eyes of all look hopefully to you,
and you give them their food in due season;
you open your hand
and satisfy the desire of every living thing.
—PSALM 145:15–16

On special occasions, my in-laws use this portion of Psalm 145 as their mealtime grace. I think it is a lovely way to teach children the words of the Bible. My husband's family has five different prayers that they use to bless the food before meals, and, over time, I have learned each of them. It says in today's Gospel that Jesus gave thanks for the five barley loaves and two fish before he distributed them to the five thousand people. I wonder if he recited Psalm 145.

2 Kings 4:42–44
Psalm 145:10–11,15–16,17–18
Ephesians 4:1–6
John 6:1–15

• ST. JOACHIM AND ST. ANNE, PARENTS OF THE VIRGIN MARY •

All these things Jesus spoke to the crowds in parables.
He spoke to them only in parables,
to fulfill what had been said through the prophet:
I will open my mouth in parables,
I will announce what has lain hidden
from the foundation of the world.
—MATTHEW 13:34–35

God is a storyteller. Think of the storytellers you have known. Your mother, perhaps? Your grandfather? Have you known a very young person who loved to tell stories? I have. My daughter Ellen would come home from school and, with a cookie and milk in hand, tell me everything that happened that day. I was delighted. Other parents would come to me to find out what was going on in the classroom. But I learned that storytelling goes both ways. Her first-grade teacher said to me, "I'm guessing that you don't have any family secrets." God doesn't have family secrets either.

Exodus 32:15–24,30–34
Psalm 106:19–20,21–22,23
Matthew 13:31–35

Merciful and gracious is the LORD,
slow to anger and abounding in kindness.
He will not always chide,
nor does he keep his wrath forever.
—PSALM 103:8–9

Someone once told me, "Beware the anger of a patient man."
I took this to mean that I should not push a patient person so
far that his sense of justice outweighs his virtue of patience.
God is like that.

Exodus 33:7–11; 34:5b–9,28
Psalm 103:6–7,8–9,10–11,12–13
Matthew 13:36–43

*When Aaron, then, and the other children
of Israel saw Moses
and noticed how radiant the skin of his face
had become,
they were afraid to come near him. . . .
When he [Moses] finished speaking with them,
he put a veil over his face.*
—EXODUS 34:30,33

After conversing with God, Moses didn't realize that his face was shining. Aaron and the Israelites were frightened by the glow coming from him, so he put a veil over his face. I have run away from shining faces as well. If someone is so exuberantly in love that it shows all over their face, it can be a bit glaring. This is why newly engaged people are teased by their friends, and it is why new grandparents are constantly imposing baby pictures on anyone who will look. Often, a person's over-the-top love is something we want to veil. The fault is in us. Moses was not the problem.

Exodus 34:29–35
Psalm 99:5,6,7,9
Matthew 13:44–46

*Jesus entered a village
where a woman whose name was Martha
welcomed him.*
—LUKE 10:38

Much has already been said about Martha being overly busy
and anxious while Mary sits at Jesus' feet and listens to him.
It's a good lesson. But verse 38 holds a lesson as well: *Jesus
entered a village where a woman whose name was Martha welcomed
him.* Martha may have become a distracted hostess, but she
was the hostess—she invited him into the house. First steps
are necessary. Today, invite Jesus into your house. Perhaps
tomorrow you will be able to sit at his feet.

Exodus 40:16–21,34–38
Psalm 84:3,4,5–6a and 8a,11
John 11:19–27 or Luke 10:38–42

Friday

JULY 30

• ST. PETER CHRYSOLOGUS, BISHOP AND DOCTOR OF THE CHURCH •

*Jesus came to his native place and taught the people
in their synagogue.
They were astonished and said,
"Where did this man get such wisdom
and mighty deeds?
Is he not the carpenter's son?"*
—MATTHEW 13:54–55A

The people of Nazareth do not dispute that Jesus has wisdom
or that he is doing mighty deeds. They are only upset that he
has an ordinary family and hails from their own village. They
reject him for being one of them. Jesus' wisdom is found in
his parables about ordinary people doing ordinary things in
villages. He rarely tells a parable about city people or
scholars. The people he heals are usually poor or ostracized.
Sometimes he heals a pagan, sometimes a child, and often
everyone in the crowd. I must remember to not reject
prophets, healers, and teachers who look like me.

Leviticus 23:1,4–11,15–16,27,34b–37
Psalm 81:3–4,5–6,10–11ab
Matthew 13:54–58

≥244≤

Prompted by her mother, she said,
"Give me here on a platter the head
of John the Baptist."
—MATTHEW 14:8

This is an awful story, but I don't recall anyone ever denying it. When people doubt the veracity of the Gospels, they don't say, "And that gruesome story about the teenager persuading the king to behead John the Baptist—how ridiculous—that would never happen." Nope. We humans all know that this is a true story because this kind of thing happens all over the world. Isn't it strange, then, that the Gospel accounts that people doubt are the feeding of the five thousand, the healing of lepers, the restoring of sight to the blind, and the resurrection of Jesus? Why do we believe in unimaginable cruelty but refuse to believe in unimaginable good? Personally, I believe the miracles are happening as often as the atrocities. Actually, *more* often.

Leviticus 25:1,8–17
Psalm 67:2–3,5,7–8
Matthew 14:1–12

So they said to him,
"What can we do to accomplish the works of God?"
Jesus answered and said to them,
"This is the work of God, that you believe
in the one he sent."
So they said to him,
"What sign can you do, that we may see
and believe in you? What can you do?"
—JOHN 6:28–30

The people ask Jesus to tell them what *to do* to work for God. But Jesus doesn't tell them to do anything: he tells them to believe in him. Apparently, that answer isn't what they want to hear, because then they ask Jesus *what he can do* to prove to them that they should believe in him. Jesus tells them again that they only have to believe. We believe in doing. We want to deserve the bread we eat, to earn salvation, and to control God's gifts. But that's not why God made us.

Exodus 16:2–4,12–15
Psalm 78:3–4,23–24,25,54(24b)
Ephesians 4:17,20–24
John 6:24–35

• ST. EUSEBIUS OF VERCELLI, BISHOP • ST. PETER JULIAN EYMARD, PRIEST •

Moses asked the LORD,
"Why are you so displeased with me
that you burden me with all this people? . . .
For they are crying to me,
'Give us meat for our food.'
I cannot carry all this people by myself,
for they are too heavy for me.
. . . please do me the favor of killing me at once,
so that I need no longer face this distress."
—NUMBERS 11:11,14,15

We have a great power to distress others merely by complaining endlessly. Right now, write down each complaint you made today. Did you complain about the weather? Did you swear at the traffic? Did someone not do their share of the housework? Are you having a bad-hair day? Is your boss unreasonable? Is your dinner delayed? Are we trying to distress people by complaining to them? No? Are you sure? Why, then, do we complain?

Numbers 11:4b–15
Psalm 81:12–13,14–15,16–17
Matthew 14:13–21

AUGUST 3

*At once Jesus spoke to them, "Take courage, it is I;
do not be afraid."
Peter said to him in reply,
"Lord, if it is you, command me to come to you
on the water."
He said, "Come."*
—MATTHEW 14:27–29A

Jesus did not ask Peter to walk on water. It was Peter who asked Jesus to "command me to come to you on the water." From time to time, I do something like this. I say to God, "Help me put on this program for the church." Or "Help me give this speech." Or "Help us raise a whole bunch of money for your work." And Jesus smiles, shrugs, and says, "Come." It is no surprise that I sink a lot.

Numbers 12:1–13
Psalm 51:3–4,5–6ab,6cd–7,12–13
Matthew 14:22–36 or 15:1–2,10–14

Wednesday
AUGUST 4

• ST. JOHN MARY VIANNEY, PRIEST •

He said in reply,
"It is not right to take the food of the children
and throw it to the dogs."
—MATTHEW 15:26

This is the most perplexing thing that Jesus ever said. He is
clearly insulting the Canaanite woman. What's more—he is
in her region, in her territory. Why in the world would he go
to Sidon and Tyre if he doesn't want to talk to Canaanites?
The geographical situation is of Jesus' making, and then he
gets nasty when the local woman asks for help? Absurd. The
end of the story is weak compared to the beginning. She
stays calm and continues to ask, and he relents and proclaims
that her faith is "great." I guess this is a lesson in the merits of
persistence, but I still struggle with it. It would be like me
driving to a ball game downtown and then acting
disrespectfully to a panhandler.

Numbers 13:1–2,25—14:1,26a–29a,34–35
Psalm 106:6–7ab,13–14,21–22,23
Matthew 15:21–28

"And so I say to you, you are Peter,
and upon this rock I will build my Church,
and the gates of the netherworld
shall not prevail against it."
—MATTHEW 16:18

He turned and said to Peter,
"Get behind me, Satan! You are an obstacle to me.
You are thinking not as God does,
but as human beings do."
—MATTHEW 16:23

Peter is given the keys to the kingdom, and within five verses
he is drop-kicked into Satan's camp. Let's look at what
happened between these verses: Jesus predicted he would be
killed by the religious leaders, and then Peter took Jesus aside
and rebuked him for telling the scary truth. Apparently the
downward path from enlightenment to hell goes through
fear. Lesson learned: do not be afraid of the truth.

Numbers 20:1–13
Psalm 95:1–2,6–7,8–9
Matthew 16:13–23

Friday

AUGUST 6

Then a cloud came, casting a shadow over them;
from the cloud came a voice,
"This is my beloved Son. Listen to him."
—MARK 9:7

In the Old Testament, God speaks from a cloud, and God does it again here. Three times in my life I have climbed a mountain considered to be sacred, a place of apparitions and enlightenment. The first time it was Bear Butte, a mountain that is holy for Native Americans. The weather was cold, and wispy clouds surrounded us as we silently walked up the winding trail. Halfway to the top we heard a sound like moaning. Was it an injured animal? Or the wind in the trees, perhaps? It seemed to come from the clouds around us. I stared at my companions, but we didn't speak. Jesus told the apostles to wait until after the Resurrection to talk about what happened on the mountain.

Daniel 7:9–10,13–14
Psalm 97:1–2,5–6,9
2 Peter 1:16–19
Mark 9:2–10

> *Then the disciples approached Jesus in private and said,*
> *"Why could we not drive it out?"*
> *He said to them, "Because of your little faith.*
> *Amen, I say to you, if you have faith the size*
> *of a mustard seed,*
> *you will say to this mountain,*
> *'Move from here to there,' and it will move.*
> *Nothing will be impossible for you."*
> —MATTHEW 17:19–20

Faith is a choice to believe what is unseen and can't be proven. Years ago, I did not want faith. I wanted to see miracles with my own eyes and be convinced by arguments that proved that Jesus is God and worthy of my faith. I did not want to trust an invisible God or believe in things that were paradoxical. The disciples saw many miracles and heard Jesus firsthand, yet their faith was little. I, like them, had to *decide* to believe.

Deuteronomy 6:4–13
Psalm 18:2–3a,3c–4,47 and 51
Matthew 17:14–20

Sunday

AUGUST 8

• NINETEENTH SUNDAY IN ORDINARY TIME •

Elijah looked and there at his head was a hearth cake
and a jug of water.
After he ate and drank, he lay down again,
but the angel of the LORD came back a second time,
touched him, and ordered,
"Get up and eat, else the journey will be too long
for you!"
—1 KINGS 19:6–7

I love this verse in the Bible. I repeat it to myself when I get weary of the everyday struggles of life: "Get up and eat, else the journey will be too long for you!" Is there a better way to say, "Take care of yourself!"? Sometimes I think that I can work without breaks, drive without resting my eyes, and be kind when I am exhausted. I can't do any of those things. God sends angels to me, as well: my doctor, my husband, my adult children, my friends, and my spiritual advisor.

1 Kings 19:4–8
Psalm 34:2–3,4–5,6–7,8–9(9a)
Ephesians 4:30—5:2
John 6:41–51

AUGUST 9

• ST. TERESA BENEDICTA OF THE CROSS, VIRGIN AND MARTYR •

When they came to Capernaum,
the collectors of the temple tax approached Peter
and said,
"Does not your teacher pay the temple tax?"
"Yes," he said.
—MATTHEW 17:24,25A

The temple tax is the money that keeps the institution of
religion afloat. If we don't pay the Bishop's Appeal, or
Propagation of the Faith, or put our envelopes in the basket
on Sunday, then the buildings will crumble, the teachers will
be laid off, and the parking lot will have potholes. Peter
answers in the affirmative, but he pays the tax only after
obeying Jesus, who works a miracle by putting the money in
a fish's mouth. Jesus doesn't act overly concerned about it.
He seems to enjoy the moment. Perhaps the best way to
collect the money is through obedience, miracles, and a
little fun?

Deuteronomy 10:12–22
Psalm 147:12–13,14–15,19–20
Matthew 17:22–27

"Whoever loves his life loses it,
and whoever hates his life in this world
will preserve it for eternal life."
—JOHN 12:25

This is hard for me to grasp. Jesus doesn't want us to hate our lives; he wants us to be full of faith, hope, and love—hardly a recipe for an unhappy life. So, what is he saying here? In the first part of the verse, he says that loving our life will result in losing it. Well, sure, that makes sense. In loving our children, we let them grow up and move away. Loving our spouse, we encourage them to grow and change the way they feel called to change. And loving ourselves, we don't allow our brains, bodies, or dreams to stagnate; we leave behind the things of the past and move forward. Perhaps he is saying not to hoard blessings but to plant them like seeds.

2 Corinthians 9:6–10
Psalm 112:1–2,5–6,7–8,9
John 12:24–26

*"Again, amen, I say to you, if two of you agree on earth
about anything for which they are to pray,
it shall be granted to them by my heavenly Father."*
—MATTHEW 18:19

Jesus repeated this statement, so it must be important. Yet do I believe it? Actually, I do believe it. The problem with most of my prayers is that I am not necessarily in agreement with my prayer partners about what to pray for. For example, we may pray for world peace, but my idea of peace is not necessarily their idea of peace. I may have in mind that all the world's resources are distributed so fairly that no one would ever think of taking up arms. My prayer partner may be praying that the rest of the world stops fighting and lets us live the way we want to live. That is not the same peace prayer.

Deuteronomy 34:1–12
Psalm 66:1–3a,5 and 8,16–17
Matthew 18:15–20

Peter approached Jesus and asked him,
"Lord, if my brother sins against me,
how often must I forgive him?
As many as seven times?"
—MATTHEW 18:21

In this story I picture Peter grinding his teeth and marching up to Jesus, fairly spitting with fury. His question doesn't seem like a casual, hypothetical sort of thing. Peter has lost his patience with someone, and now he wants Jesus to tell him that it's okay to stop putting up with the nonsense. Jesus doesn't let him off the hook, however. The odd thing about Jesus' parable is that, in the end, the master hands over the offender to the torturers. What was the unforgivable man's offense? The original debt? Nope. The master punished him because the man failed to forgive another person. It's not our mistakes, sins, or offenses that doom us: it's our unforgiveness.

Joshua 3:7–10a,11,13–17
Psalm 114:1–2,3–4,5–6
Matthew 18:21—19:1

• ST. PONTIAN, POPE, AND ST. HIPPOLYTUS, PRIEST, MARTYRS •

Some Pharisees approached Jesus,
and tested him, saying,
"Is it lawful for a man to divorce his wife
for any cause whatever?"
—MATTHEW 19:3

The Pharisees again ask a loaded question to test Jesus. What other questions have they asked? "Is it lawful to pay tribute to Caesar?" "This woman was caught in the very act of adultery and the law says to stone her. What do you say?" "Why are you doing what is unlawful on the Sabbath?" "Who is my neighbor?" "Tell us, by what authority are you doing these things?" Jesus taught mercy: It is lawful to pay taxes; it is not lawful to stone people for adultery; it is lawful to cure on the Sabbath; we are all neighbors; and Jesus has God's authority. Jesus' answer is that Moses's law concerning divorce was counteracting something worse. Jesus wants mercy, always mercy. Go, then, and do the same.

Joshua 24:1–13
Psalm 136:1–3,16–18,21–22 and 24
Matthew 19:3–12

Saturday

AUGUST 14

• ST. MAXIMILLIAN KOLBE, PRIEST AND MARTYR •

*Children were brought to Jesus
that he might lay his hands on them and pray.*
—MATTHEW 19:13

I assume that it was mothers and fathers who brought the children to Jesus, and perhaps grandparents and aunts and uncles as well. We can still do this. He wants us to do this. Our prayers bring the children before Jesus. Pray with joy and confidence that Jesus is delighted when you lift the children up to him. Ask simply for his blessing, and you may be confident that you are doing God's will exactly.

Joshua 24:14–29
Psalm 16:1–2a and 5,7–8,11
Matthew 19:13–15

Sunday

AUGUST 15

• THE ASSUMPTION OF THE BLESSED VIRGIN MARY •

> *Then another sign appeared in the sky;*
> *it was a huge red dragon, with seven heads*
> *and ten horns,*
> *and on its heads were seven diadems.*
> *Its tail swept away a third of the stars in the sky*
> *and hurled them down to the earth.*
> *Then the dragon stood before the woman*
> *about to give birth,*
> *to devour her child when she gave birth.*
> —REVELATION 12:3–4

I gave birth to our first child, Ellen Marie, on this date. This reading about the woman giving birth and having her child swept up to God and the woman fleeing into the desert is a little unsettling for me. I have no idea what the book of Revelation is trying to reveal to us, and that's a good thing. I can highly recommend that you go to Mass today and listen to the homilist's explanation.

VIGIL:	DAY:
1 Chronicles 15:3–4,15–16; 16:1–2	Revelation 11:19a; 12:1–6a,10ab
Psalm 132:6–7,9–10,13–14	Psalm 45:10,11,12,16
1 Corinthians 15:54b–57	1 Corinthians 15:20–27
Luke 11:27–28	Luke 1:39–56

Jesus said to him, "If you wish to be perfect, go,
sell what you have and give to the poor,
and you will have treasure in heaven.
Then come, follow me."
—MATTHEW 19:21

This is clear instruction on how to be perfect. I'm not yet ready to sell what I have and give it to the poor. First, I would like to follow Jesus and get used to the idea a little at a time. But Jesus doesn't put it in that order. Perfection is within my grasp; I just don't want to go that far yet. Someone once told me that artisans are people who do their craft beyond what is reasonable. A perfect Christian isn't reasonable either.

Judges 2:11–19
Psalm 106:34–35,36–37,39–40,43ab and 44
Matthew 19:16–22

AUGUST 17

"*And everyone who has given up houses*
or brothers or sisters
or father or mother or children or lands
for the sake of my name will receive
a hundred times more,
and will inherit eternal life.
But many who are first will be last,
and the last will be first."
—MATTHEW 19:29–30

Through St. Vincent de Paul, when I meet someone who has
no home, no family, no savings, or no job and listen to their
story of loss, I often find out that they still help other people
whenever they are able. They have lost much, but they have
not lost kindness and love. Of course they will be first in
God's kingdom. It makes perfect sense to me.

Judges 6:11–24a
Psalm 85:9,11–12,13–14
Matthew 19:23–30

Great is his glory in your victory;
majesty and splendor you conferred upon him.
For you made him a blessing forever;
you gladdened him with the joy of your face.
—PSALM 21:6–7

Picture "the joy of God's face." Close your eyes and slowly grow a smile on your lips, raise your cheeks slightly, and lift your chin. Jesus is a young man in his thirties. He has clear, bright eyes and wavy hair. He is delighted to see you, absolutely delighted. He hasn't seen you in many months, and he has so much to tell you. But first, he wants to hear about your soul—what adventures have moved your heart this year? He is so very pleased to sit still in front of you and listen. "Great is his glory in your victory." He is waiting to share his joy in your victory—tell him about it.

Judges 9:6–15
Psalm 21:2–3,4–5,6–7
Matthew 20:1–16

Thursday

AUGUST 19

• ST. JOHN EUDES, PRIEST •

Sacrifice or oblation you wished not,
but ears open to obedience you gave me.
Burnt offerings or sin-offerings you sought not;
then said I, "Behold I come."
—PSALM 40:7–8A

In the first reading today, Jephthah pledges to sacrifice another person in order to honor God. God is not requesting this sacrifice. It is Jephthah's will, not God's. Jephthah keeps the vow anyway and sacrifices his daughter. What Jephthah should have sacrificed was his own vow, his own will, not his daughter's life. We still do this today. We sacrifice the lives of others because we have made vows to the government, our employers, public opinion, and even religion. Any promise I make to God I must examine honestly to understand who will bear the sacrifice more: me or someone else?

Judges 11:29–39a
Psalm 40:5,7–8a,8b–9,10
Matthew 22:1–14

When the Pharisees heard that Jesus had
silenced the Sadducees,
they gathered together, and one of them,
a scholar of the law, tested him by asking,
"Teacher, which commandment in the law
is the greatest?"
—MATTHEW 22:34–36

This kind of questioning annoys me. The Pharisees are trying to trip Jesus up. They know the answer to the question, and they intend to find fault in whatever Jesus tells them. We Christians do this too. We ask things like, "Do you know the salvation that comes from baptism?" or "Have you been saved?" or "Do you know why God made you?" They are setups. We are not trying to love God and love our neighbor; we are trying to make converts. Some people think that is the same thing. I find it insincere. Only love will make lovers of God and neighbor. Arguments will make people who are just like us.

Ruth 1:1,3–6,14b–16,22
Psalm 146:5–6ab,6c–7,8–9a,9bc–10
Matthew 22:34–40

*"He will be your comfort and the support of your old age,
for his mother is the daughter-in-law who loves you.
She is worth more to you than seven sons!"*
—RUTH 4:15

The story of Ruth tells of an outsider, a Moabite, who
marries into an Israelite family and sticks with them through
the death of her husband. She does this because she loves her
mother-in-law, Naomi, and won't abandon her. Ruth ends up
becoming the grandmother of the greatest king in Israel,
King David. God loves to choose the outsiders, the converts,
the youngest, the poor, the widows, and the orphans. If you
are any of these, have hope: "You are worth more than
seven sons!"

Ruth 2:1–3,8–11; 4:13–17
Psalm 128:1b–2,3,4,5
Matthew 23:1–12

Sunday

AUGUST 22

• TWENTY-FIRST SUNDAY IN ORDINARY TIME •

Jesus then said to the Twelve, "Do you also want to leave?"
—JOHN 6:67

We can leave our jobs, and the consequences sometimes fall
on our family and coworkers. We can leave our homeland,
especially if it becomes dangerous, but we will end up in
someone else's homeland. We can leave our wife or husband,
although it is wrenching to many people, not only ourselves.
We can abandon our children and inflict untold damage on
their psyches. And we can leave the church. In this passage,
Jesus asks his friends if they are going to leave him. God
gives us the freedom to leave God. This is free will. We can
leave or we can stay. Both are powerful, and our decision
affects many people besides ourselves.

Joshua 24:1–2a,15–17,18b
Psalm 34:2–3,16–17,18–19,20–21,22–23(9a)
Ephesians 5:21–32 or 5:2a,25–32
John 6:60–69

Jesus said to the crowds and to his disciples:
"Woe to you, scribes and Pharisees, you hypocrites.
You lock the Kingdom of heaven before men.
You do not enter yourselves,
nor do you allow entrance to those trying to enter."
—MATTHEW 23:13–14

How do I lock people out of God's kingdom? God's kingdom is within me, just as it is within each of us. It is entirely within my power to keep people out by simply refusing to engage with them. The kingdom of God is like a mustard seed. I can refuse to let the mustard seed grow into a plant where birds build their nests by keeping it as an exclusive home for only those who follow the rules. The kingdom of God is like a woman who lost a coin. I can lock people out by letting the coin stay lost.

1 Thessalonians 1:1–5,8b–10
Psalm 149:1b–2,3–4,5–6a and 9b
Matthew 23:13–22

*Philip found Nathanael and told him,
"We have found the one about whom
Moses wrote in the law,
and also the prophets, Jesus son of Joseph,
from Nazareth."
But Nathanael said to him,
"Can anything good come from Nazareth?"
Philip said to him, "Come and see."*
—JOHN 1:45–46

This is a pretty good example of what it is like to invite people to church. We might say, "Would you like to come with me to Mass (or Bible study, or the ladies' brunch)?" and we get suspicion, rolled eyes, or a big sigh. Can't you picture Nathanael making a face when he says, "Can anything good come from Nazareth?" Have hope and keep inviting, as Philip did.

Revelation 21:9b–14
Psalm 145:10–11,12–13,17–18
John 1:45–51

Wednesday

AUGUST 25

• ST. LOUIS • ST. JOSEPH CALASANZ, PRIEST •

Where can I go from your spirit?
From your presence where can I hide?
If I go up to the heavens, you are there;
if I sink to the nether world, you are present there.
—PSALM 139:7–8

The psalmist is saying that God is everywhere. We know this, but we don't think about it in terms of hiding or fleeing from God the way these verses tell it. When do I flee from God? When I'm angry? No, I share that with God. When I am confused? No, I run to God with that. I usually *seek* God in loneliness, joy, and sorrow. I *flee* from God when I just want to do something the way I think it should be done no matter what other people prefer. When do you flee from God?

1 Thessalonians 2:9–13
Psalm 139:7–8,9–10,11–12ab
Matthew 23:27–32

AUGUST 26

Jesus said to his disciples:
"Stay awake!
For you do not know on which day your Lord will come."
—MATTHEW 24:42

I am a morning person. I love to jump out of bed at the break
of dawn or even before sunrise and get the day started. My
energy lasts until about three in the afternoon, and then, if
something needs to be addressed or I'm supposed to call
someone or write something, it's too late. Anything that
requires alertness must be put off until the next day. My least
favorite holidays are New Year's Eve and Halloween. I am
yawning when the fun begins. When Jesus says, "Stay
awake," I am dismayed. On Easter he came in the morning.
I'm hoping he stays consistent with his second coming.

1 Thessalonians 3:7–13
Psalm 90:3–5a,12–13,14 and 17
Matthew 24:42–51

Light dawns for the just;
and gladness, for the upright of heart.
—PSALM 97:11

St. Monica is put forward to us as an example of an unflagging woman of prayer. She prayed for the salvation of her son, Augustine, and he gave her the credit when he put aside his unbelief and converted to Catholicism. This is nice. But I don't think God blames mothers whose children do not convert. We all are given free will, and even a mother's prayers are not strong enough to negate that gift. Monica was a good mom, but so are the moms who never see the answer to their prayers. All you moms reading this, take Psalm 97:11 to heart: "Light dawns for the just; and gladness for the upright of heart." It is a promise for both you and your children.

1 Thessalonians 4:1–8
Psalm 97:1 and 2b,5–6,10,11–12
Matthew 25:1–13

AUGUST 28

• ST. AUGUSTINE, BISHOP AND DOCTOR OF THE CHURCH •

*[Y]ou yourselves have been taught by God
to love one another. . . .
Nevertheless we urge you, brothers and sisters,
to progress even more,
and to aspire to live a tranquil life,
to mind your own affairs,
and to work with your own hands,
as we instructed you.*

—1 THESSALONIANS 4:9B, 10B–11

Paul writes that they already know how to love. He advises them to live a quiet life. Has anyone ever told you that you already know how to love? Has anyone told you to work with your hands? Or that it's progress to mind your own affairs? Me neither. Our culture is so competitive that we are never told we are good enough. We are urged to do more, work harder, experience more, achieve, and acquire. Paul believes in the Thessalonians as they are. He doesn't doubt their love. Listen to Paul.

1 Thessalonians 4:9–11
Psalm 98:1,7–8,9
Matthew 25:14–30

Religion that is pure and undefiled before God
and the Father is this:
to care for orphans and widows in their affliction
and to keep oneself unstained by the world.
—JAMES 1:27

Religion has a bad name in the world. All religion, not just
Catholicism. It is widely believed and taught that religion
promotes intolerance, violence, and wars. Even some people
who practice various religious beliefs will at times spread this
misinformation about religions other than their own: "My
religion is not violent, but theirs is." Way back in the infancy
of Christianity, the letter of James advises how to keep
religion undefiled: care for the orphans and widows, and
don't do nasty stuff like you see in the world. It is a
nondefensive, nonaggressive posture, like the way
Jesus lived.

Deuteronomy 4:1–2,6–8
Psalm 15:2–3,3–4,4–5(1a)
James 1:17–18,21b–22,27
Mark 7:1–8,14–15,21–23

We do not want you to be unaware, brother and sisters,
about those who have fallen asleep,
so that you may not grieve like the rest,
who have no hope.
—1 THESSALONIANS 4:13

Thessalonians is often read at funerals. I find it comforting to be reminded that we will be reunited with our loved ones in the next section of life. Everlasting life was shown to us by Jesus' resurrection and subsequent appearances afterward, but that isn't all the evidence we have. When I wrote the book *The Prayer List*, many people told me their stories about the next life. Some heard voices, some watched their dying loved ones talk with others who had gone on ahead, and one even told me about his daughter coming back to this life. If you have a story, don't be afraid to share it. It may be a comfort for others.

1 Thessalonians 4:13–18
Psalm 96:1 and 3,4–5,11–12,13
Luke 4:16–30

AUGUST 31

For God did not destine us for wrath,
but to gain salvation through our Lord Jesus Christ,
who died for us, so that whether we are
awake or asleep
we may live together with him.
—1 THESSALONIANS 5:9–10

God isn't mad at you: "God did not destine us for wrath."
Paul writes that God wants to live with you, both now and in
the next life. Get over the idea that God might be
disappointed in you. Is a father disappointed in his
two-year-old child when she is naughty? No. The father
chuckles or sighs, picks up the child, and distracts her from
what she is doing. In God's eyes we are like lovable toddlers
who need watching and teaching. No matter how you
messed up, God isn't mad at you even a little bit. So, laugh
and love.

1 Thessalonians 5:1–6,9–11
Psalm 27:1,4,13–14
Luke 4:31–37

SEPTEMBER 1

At daybreak, Jesus left and went to a deserted place.
The crowds went looking for him, and when they
came to him,
they tried to prevent him from leaving them.
—LUKE 4:42

The people of Capernaum didn't want Jesus to go to other places to preach and heal. He had preached in their synagogue the day before, then healed all their sick and afflicted that evening. In the morning he went off to be alone, and they searched for him. The people wanted him to stay in their little town and be their own personal healer and preacher. We still act this way. If our parish priest is asked to move to another parish, we send letters to the bishop. Even if our priest is asked to help out in another town, we get annoyed that he isn't available when we want him. We can be more generous than this.

Colossians 1:1–8
Psalm 52:10,11
Luke 4:38–44

SEPTEMBER 2

Jesus said to Simon, "Do not be afraid;
from now on you will be catching men."
—LUKE 5:10B

Jesus has a sense of humor here. Simon is terrified by the
large catch of fish and begs Jesus to depart from him. Jesus
tells them that fish are nothing: just wait until they start
catching men. Can you picture Simon Peter's face when Jesus
says this? Jaw-drop astonishment. Now, stop a moment. You
do realize that Jesus is saying the same thing to all of us,
don't you?

Colossians 1:9–14
Psalm 98:2–3ab,3cd–4,5–6
Luke 5:1–11

Brothers and sisters:
Christ Jesus is the image of the invisible God,
the firstborn of all creation.
—COLOSSIANS 1:15

When we see Jesus, we see God. When we hear Jesus, we hear God. When we love Jesus, we love God. This is what it means to be a Christian. Can people of other faiths or no faith see, hear, and love God? Yes. Who are we to limit God? God is the father of everyone and, being God, can be present wherever and to whomever God wishes. Believing in God's omnipotent love is what it means to be a Christian as well. To be humble and just, loving all God's children, and loving God more than ourselves is the essence of Christianity. Jesus shows us, tells us, and loves us. We are called to seek him, listen to him, and imitate him.

Colossians 1:15–20
Psalm 100:1b–2,3,4,5
Luke 5:33–39

SEPTEMBER 4

*Then he said to them, "The Son of Man
is lord of the sabbath."*
—LUKE 6:5

Jesus is telling the Pharisees, who are serious rule followers,
that he is in charge of the rules. I have been a student, and I
have been a teacher, and I am one of those people who loves
to follow rules. I despise classrooms where no one seems to
be in charge. I want order. In my way of thinking, if everyone
followed the same rules, then there would be no arguments,
no misbehavior, and no chaos. Probably, if I had been
listening to this exchange between Jesus and the Pharisees, I
would have sided with the Pharisees. I guess this means that
Jesus still needs to convert me to following him, not the
rules. But I like rules. I have a way to go.

Colossians 1:21–23
Psalm 54:3–4,6 and 8
Luke 6:1–5

SEPTEMBER 5

• TWENTY-THIRD SUNDAY IN ORDINARY TIME •

He ordered them not to tell anyone.
But the more he ordered them not to,
the more they proclaimed it.
—MARK 7:36

You have to love human nature. Jesus tells us at the end of
the Gospels to go out and proclaim his kingdom to the entire
world, and we have been hampered by programs, systems,
hierarchies, and all manner of human ambition and foibles
ever since. But here, Jesus tells the people to keep his
miracles to themselves, and they go blab it everywhere.
What will you do when I repeat in bold print at the end of
this meditation, **Do not tell anyone about God's miracles in
your life?**

Isaiah 35:4–7a
Psalm 146:6–7,8–9,9–10(1b)
James 2:1–5
Mark 7:31–37

Only in God be at rest, my soul,
for from him comes my hope.
He only is my rock and my salvation,
my stronghold: I shall not be disturbed.
—PSALM 62:6–7

I can rest my body in bed, in a comfy chair, on a beach, on a church pew, in an airplane, or even on a bicycle. There are many places where the tiredness sloughs off me and I am rejuvenated by simply resting my feet. There is only one place where I can rest my soul. Soul rest is rest from worry, fear, and guilt. Soul rest is achieved through trusting God.

Colossians 1:24—2:3
Psalm 62:6–7,9
Luke 6:6–11

SEPTEMBER 7

See to it that no one captivate you with an empty,
seductive philosophy
according to the tradition of men,
according to the elemental powers of the world
and not according to Christ.
—COLOSSIANS 2:8

What are these empty, seductive philosophies of which Paul writes? Probably most of the "isms." Think about all the words you know that end with "ism" and write them down one at a time. Don't stop until you have at least ten. Have you bought into any of the philosophies that they promote? I'm not going to name them here because the ones that come to my mind are the ones that seduce me. The ones that come to your mind are the ones you should look at cautiously.

Colossians 2:6–15
Psalm 145:1b–2,8–9,10–11
Luke 6:12–19

SEPTEMBER 8

• THE NATIVITY OF THE BLESSED VIRGIN MARY •

Let me sing of the LORD, "He has been good to me."
—PSALM 13:6C

Mary always thought that God had been good to her. God asked her to become pregnant when she wasn't yet married, to give birth in a barn, to flee into exile, and, ultimately, to watch her only son be tortured and executed. But nowhere does Scripture or tradition record that Mary took any of this as a curse or misfortune. She was so sure of God's love that no matter what happened, she trusted that it was all coming out right. She is the kind of teacher we need.

Micah 5:1–4a or Romans 8:28–30
Psalm 13:6ab,6c
Matthew 1:1–16,18–23 or 1:18–23

SEPTEMBER 9

• ST. PETER CLAVER, PRIEST •

And let the peace of Christ control your hearts,
the peace into which you were also called
in one Body.
And be thankful.
—COLOSSIANS 3:15

Let the peace of Christ control my heart? I would love it if this were true. My heart is restless, especially at night. I think about the things I said during the day that I probably should not have said. I think about the work I left undone. My heart weeps for the people I know who are struggling with illnesses. Watching the news makes me worry about the future. Not watching the news makes me worry that I am not shouldering my adult responsibility to be informed. It all works together to upset my heart's peace. At times I cry out, "Lord, protect my thought processes!" Surprisingly, this does work. And I am thankful.

Colossians 3:12–17
Psalm 150:1b–2,3–4,5–6
Luke 6:27–38

*Paul, an Apostle of Christ Jesus by command
of God our savior
and of Christ Jesus our hope,
to Timothy, my true child in faith:
grace, mercy, and peace from God the Father
and Christ Jesus our Lord.*
—1 TIMOTHY 1:1–2

This is how Paul addresses his letter to Timothy. Wouldn't you love to receive a letter like this? Imagine opening an envelope from your pastor, or your spiritual director, or maybe from a former teacher, and reading the first line that affirms that you are their "true child in faith." Is there someone you can write to, or text, and begin with *My true child in faith?*

1 Timothy 1:1–2,12–14
Psalm 16:1b–2a and 5,7–8,11
Luke 6:39–42

Beloved:
This saying is trustworthy and deserves full acceptance:
Christ Jesus came into the world to save sinners.
Of these I am the foremost.
But for that reason I was mercifully treated,
so that in me, as the foremost,
Christ Jesus might display all his patience
as an example
for those who would come to believe in him
for everlasting life.
—1 TIMOTHY 1:15–16

Paul seems to be saying that he was chosen by Christ
precisely because he was such a terrible sinner. Paul's sins
gave Jesus a way to show people how incredibly merciful
God is. This is enough to keep each of us from being proud
of our position as Christians. He called us not because we are
good but because we are wretched.

1 Timothy 1:15–17
Psalm 113:1b–2,3–4,5a and 6–7
Luke 6:43–49

If a brother or sister has nothing to wear
and has no food for the day,
and one of you says to them,
"Go in peace, keep warm, and eat well,"
but you do not give them the necessities of the body,
"what good is it?"
So also faith of itself,
if it does not have works, is dead.
—JAMES 2:15–17

Apparently, faith can die. We sometimes fear that faith in God dies when we don't go to Mass every Sunday, or if we don't evangelize, or if other people commit sins. But that isn't how faith dies. Faith lives when we stop for a stranded motorist even if we miss Mass because of it. Faith lives no matter what religion we belong to, no matter what sins we have committed. Our faith lives when we help. Faith dies when we don't help. James tells us how to keep faith alive.

Isaiah 50:5–9a
Psalm 116:1–2,3–4,5–6,8–9(9)
James 2:14–18
Mark 8:27–35

• ST. JOHN CHRYSOSTOM, BISHOP AND DOCTOR OF THE CHURCH •

Beloved:
First of all, I ask that supplications, prayers,
petitions, and thanksgivings be offered for everyone,
for kings and for all in authority,
that we may lead a quiet and tranquil life
in all devotion and dignity.
This is good and pleasing to God our savior,
who wills everyone to be saved
and to come to knowledge of the truth.
—1 TIMOTHY 2:1–4

God wills everyone to be saved. Yes, even the terrorists, the despots, the abusers, and the worst sinners you can think of. This is why we don't believe in war or the death penalty as a way to achieve justice. In this letter to Timothy, Paul asks for prayers for those in authority. Remember that these people in authority executed Jesus and were persecuting his followers. Today, pray for the political and religious leaders no matter what. No exceptions.

1 Timothy 2:1–8
Psalm 28:2,7,8–9
Luke 7:1–10

SEPTEMBER 14

• THE EXALTATION OF THE HOLY CROSS •

"And just as Moses lifted up the serpent in the desert,
so must the Son of Man be lifted up,
so that everyone who believes in him
may have eternal life."
—JOHN 3:14–15

When I lift up an object, it is because I want people to see it.
If I hang a picture on the wall of my house, then I am hoping
people will look at it. What is more, I hope they will be
delighted—I do not want to disgust them. The things I put in
drawers and on lower shelves are the things I don't want
others to notice. Look around your home and notice what
you have lifted up. Are they beautiful things?
Remembrances? Healing things, perhaps?

Numbers 21:4b–9
Psalm 78:1bc–2,34–35,36–37,38
Philippians 2:6–11
John 3:13–17

Beloved:
I am writing to you,
although I hope to visit you soon.
—1 TIMOTHY 3:14

These are words from a letter of Paul to Timothy, but they could easily be from God to any of us. God gave us the Scriptures to read, but what he really wants to do is visit us. Sometimes a letter is all we have on a given day. Sometimes, we don't have the peace of mind, or the time, or the place to sit down quietly and visit with God in person. Then, the written word will have to suffice. But try to remember that God wants to visit with you in person.

1 Timothy 3:14–16
Psalm 111:1–2,3–4,5–6
John 19:25–27 or Luke 2:33–35

SEPTEMBER 16

[Jesus said], "Two people were in debt to a certain creditor;
one owed five hundred days' wages
and the other owed fifty.
Since they were unable to repay the debt,
he forgave it for both.
Which of them will love him more?"
Simon said in reply,
"The one, I suppose, whose larger debt was forgiven."
He said to him, "You have judged rightly."
—LUKE 7:41–43

Do you know of someone who is a bigger sinner than you
are? When God forgives them, it is highly likely that they
will love God more than you love God. Loving God and
loving our neighbor is what this life is all about. That is
something to think about.

1 Timothy 4:12–16
Psalm 111:7–8,9,10
Luke 7:36–50

Accompanying him were the Twelve
and some women who had been cured of evil spirits
and infirmities,
Mary, called Magdalene, from whom
seven demons had gone out,
Joanna, the wife of Herod's steward Chuza,
Susanna, and many others
who provided for them out of their resources.
—LUKE 8:1B,2–3

Jesus took not only twelve *male* friends with him through Israel;
women were part of his evangelization mission as well. I
wonder if Jesus taught the women while he taught the Twelve?
Nowhere is it written that Jesus split the crowds up into male
and female sections. I wonder if Joanna, the wife of Herod's
steward, had to get permission from her husband to follow
Jesus around? At any rate, her devotion likely made Chuza's
work life uncomfortable. Notice who financed everything.
Nothing is in the Scriptures by mistake.

1 Timothy 6:2c–12
Psalm 49:6–7,8–10,17–18,19–20
Luke 8:1–3

SEPTEMBER 18

Know that the LORD is God;
he made us, his we are;
his people, the flock he tends.
—PSALM 100:3

We belong to God, and all our problems belong to him as
well. Like sheep, we can take our overgrown fleece to our
shepherd and he will trim it. Not only will he make our
burdensome coat lighter, but also he will use the trimmed
wool for the good of others. Don't be afraid of the Shepherd.
Give him everything that weighs you down. He and his
helpers will wash it, card it, spin it, knit it, and make a
beautiful garment.

1 Timothy 6:13–16
Psalm 100:1b–2,3,4,5
Luke 8:4–15

Beloved:
Where jealousy and selfish ambition exist,
there is disorder and every foul practice.
—JAMES 3:16

Jealousy and selfish ambition are both fairly common. Most novels, movies, or plays have a character who has one or both of these flaws. A piece of drama doesn't work well if there is no conflict—conflict between the characters or conflict between a character and the society or the authorities. So, here is the lesson: If I don't want to live in constant drama, if I don't want my life to be farce or tragedy, then the jealousy and the selfish ambition in my character need to be eliminated. Then I can step off the stage and into real life.

Wisdom 2:12,17–20
Psalm 54:3–4,5,6–8(6b)
James 3:16—4:3
Mark 9:30–37

• ST. ANDREW KIM TAE-GŎN, PRIEST, AND ST. PAUL CHŎNG HA-SANG, AND
COMPANIONS, MARTYRS •

Jesus said to the crowd:
"No one who lights a lamp conceals it with a vessel
or sets it under a bed;
rather, he places it on a lampstand
so that those who enter may see the light."
—LUKE 8:16

While I was reading this Scripture passage, my cell phone
bleeped, letting me know a message had come through. If I
had not been so easily distracted, I would have ignored it,
but I looked at the screen. A woman I had been praying for
typed the results of her recent MRI and doctor visit. The
doctor told her, "I don't know what you are doing, but you're
fine—no surgery for you." She had asked me to pray with her
that she would not need more surgery. Alleluia! I'm putting
this lamp on the highest lampstand I have. Enjoy the light.

Ezra 1:1–6
Psalm 126:1b–2ab,2cd–3,4–5,6
Luke 8:16–18

SEPTEMBER 21

• ST. MATTHEW, APOSTLE AND EVANGELIST •

While he [Jesus] was at table in his [Matthew's] house,
many tax collectors and sinners came
and sat with Jesus and his disciples.
—MATTHEW 9:10

Matthew, the despised tax collector, invites Jesus and his disciples to his home, and Matthew's friends and colleagues are invited as well. Of course, who else would have a house full of sinners for Jesus to meet and talk with? It occurs to me that Jesus may have invited us to be his friends not only for ourselves but also because he wants to meet our other friends. The hope is that if anyone knows us, they may also see a glimpse of Jesus. In this sense, we are all evangelists unaware.

Ephesians 4:1–7,11–13
Psalm 19:2–3,4–5
Matthew 9:9–13

SEPTEMBER 22

He said to them, "Take nothing for the journey,
neither walking stick, nor sack, nor food, nor money,
and let no one take a second tunic."
—LUKE 9:3

It's as if Jesus is saying, "No programs, alright? Please, don't plan any programs. People don't want to be 'a member of the intended audience.' However, they do like to be visited, so just go visit them."

Ezra 9:5–9
Tobit 13:2,3–4a,4befghn,7–8
Luke 9:1–6

SEPTEMBER 23

• ST. PIUS OF PIETRELCINA, PRIEST •

But Herod said, "John I beheaded.
Who then is this about whom I hear such things?"
And he kept trying to see him.
—LUKE 9:9

Herod was the tetrarch. He had plenty of servants, soldiers, spies, and money. Doesn't it seem strange that he kept trying to see Jesus but never succeeded until the very end of Jesus' life? Jesus spoke in public and traveled widely; no need for tickets or club membership to see or hear him. Curiosity about God and spiritual things is not enough to make God visible. Fear of God and spiritual things is not going to work either. Herod was not interested in being Jesus' friend, student, or enemy. He was curious, and a little fearful, and he never heard Jesus until it was too late. Jesus says, "Don't be afraid." He means it.

Haggai 1:1–8
Psalm 149:1b–2,3–4,5–6a and 9b
Luke 9:7–9

> He said, "The Son of Man must suffer greatly
> and be rejected by the elders, the chief priest,
> and the scribes,
> and be killed and on the third day be raised."
> —LUKE 9:22

Imagine for a minute that the pastor of your church stands at the pulpit and asks for volunteers for a new project. He says, "We need a few committed people who are willing to help get this thing off the ground. It will require a couple of hours of your time each week, prayer, and perhaps a small monetary contribution." Next, suppose you sign up and the pastor confides in you this way: "I'm happy you will be part of this. I will suffer greatly and be rejected by most of the leaders of the church, and it is likely I will be executed. But don't worry—it will all turn out fine in the end." Are you still in?

Haggai 2:1–9
Psalm 43:1,2,3,4
Luke 9:18–22

SEPTEMBER 25

Jesus said to his disciples,
"Pay attention to what I am telling you.
The Son of Man is to be handed over to men."
But they did not understand this saying;
its meaning was hidden from them
so that they should not understand it,
and they were afraid to ask him about this saying.
—LUKE 9:44–45

I am not under the illusion that things are any different now.
We do not understand the meaning of much of what Jesus
said. You and I are reading Bible passages every day, but
reading words doesn't mean that we understand them.
Perhaps, if the disciples had not been afraid to ask Jesus
about his difficult saying, they would have been aware of
what was happening around them. Try to make a practice of
praying before reading Scripture, and praying after as well.
Jesus wants us to ask him about all the things he said.

Zechariah 2:5–9,14–15a
Jeremiah 31:10, 11–12ab,13
Luke 9:43b–45

But Moses answered him,
"Are you jealous for my sake?
Would that all the people of the LORD were prophets!
Would that the LORD might bestow his spirit on them all!"
—NUMBERS 11:29

Jesus replied, "Do not prevent him.
There is no one who performs a mighty deed in my name
who can at the same time speak ill of me.
For whoever is not against us is for us."
—MARK 9:39–40

Both Moses and Jesus are telling their followers, "We are not snooty." Go, and do the same.

Numbers 11:25–29
Psalm 19:8,10,12–13,14(9a)
James 5:1–6
Mark 9:38–43,45,47–48

Thus says the LORD of hosts: Old men and old women,
each with staff in hand because of old age,
shall again sit in the streets of Jerusalem.
The city shall be filled with boys and girls
playing in its streets.
—ZECHARIAH 8:4–5

St. Vincent de Paul wrote, "Let us seek out the poorest and most abandoned among us, and recognize before God that they are our lords and masters, and that we are unworthy of rendering our little services for them." The vision of St. Vincent is like the vision of Zechariah: a city restored, populated with the old and the young, all safely abiding in the streets. For this reason, we Vincentians go into the cities, visiting people in their homes, bringing help and love. We are "unworthy" to be serving them, but we have this vision of the peaceful Jerusalem, and we long to be part of it.

Zechariah 8:1–8
Psalm 102:16–18,19–21,29 and 22–23
Luke 9:46–50

SEPTEMBER 28

When the disciples James and John saw this they asked,
"Lord, do you want us to call down fire from heaven
to consume them?"
Jesus turned and rebuked them,
and they journeyed to another village.
—LUKE 9:54–56

Apparently, not only does Jesus not need any help judging people, he doesn't need any of our help in punishing them either. He does need our help, however. He needs us to be his tenderness in the world. Our hands are his when we caress, when we feed, when we bless, and when we welcome. Our hands are not his when we punish, strike, humiliate, or lock out.

Zechariah 8:20–23
Psalm 87:1b–3,4–5,6–7
Luke 9:51–56

SEPTEMBER 29

• ST. MICHAEL, ST. GABRIEL, AND ST. RAPHAEL, ARCHANGELS •

I will give thanks to you, O LORD, with all my heart,
for you have heard the words of my mouth;
in the presence of the angels I will sing your praise;
—PSALM 138:1

I have three funerals to attend this week. This happens often
because I live in the same town where I grew up and where
my parents lived, and my grandparents lived as well. My
husband reads the obituaries every evening, so we don't miss
the news of someone going on ahead. Some of my friends
moved here from far away, so when there is a death in their
hometown, they send cards and wire flowers. I, on the other
hand, bake casseroles and deliver coolers full of beer and soft
drinks. Angels do both. They send comfort from far away
and silently sit close by with a drink in hand. We are always
in the angels' presence.

Daniel 7:9–10,13–14 or Revelation 12:7–12a
Psalm 138:1–2ab,2cde–3,4–5
John 1:47–51

Jesus appointed seventy-two other disciples
whom he sent ahead of him in pairs
to every town and place he intended to visit.
—LUKE 10:1

Jesus sends us ahead of him to the places he intends to visit.
Today, when you meet a panhandler on the street, know that
you have been sent ahead of Jesus to bring hope to this
person. Later, when you go to whatever meeting, remember
that Jesus will follow you into that room. If you visit a sick
person, you are not the healer—Jesus is the healer—but you
have been sent ahead to prepare their hearts for Jesus' touch.
Everything we do, everyone we speak with, is preparation for
what Jesus is going to do and say today. Don't be worried
that it is all on your shoulders; it's not. Jesus sends us in pairs
so this will be clear.

Nehemiah 8:1–4a,5–6,7b–12
Psalm 19:8,9,10,11
Luke 10:1–12

Friday

OCTOBER 1

Remember not against us the iniquities of the past;
may your compassion quickly come to us,
for we are brought very low.
—PSALM 79:8

The psalms are often laments over past sins and pleas for God's mercy. It's almost as if there is a pattern here: we sin, things take a turn for the worse, we beg God's forgiveness, God forgives, and we praise God. Then, we sin again. Okay. If this is the way things repeat, not only in our own life but in generations of lives over millennia, then it is no wonder that God wants us to quickly get over the guilt, learn from mistakes, and move upward. Thérèse of Lisieux wrote, "When we yield to discouragement or despair, it is usually because we think too much about the past and the future." If you are feeling regretful over long-ago mistakes, stop it.

Baruch 1:15–22
Psalm 79:1b–2,3–5,8,9
Luke 10:13–16

Saturday

OCTOBER 2

• THE HOLY GUARDIAN ANGELS •

"See that you do not despise one of these little ones, for I say to you that their angels in heaven always look upon the face of my heavenly Father."
—MATTHEW 18:10

It's a comfort to know that God has angels appointed especially for children. Clearly, Jesus held the little ones in high regard, so we know that God does too. May we see children as their heavenly Father does, every day.

Baruch 4:5–12,27–29
Psalm 69:33–35,36–37
Matthew 18:1–5,10

"Therefore what God has joined together,
no human being must separate."
—MARK 10:9

Divorce is always, always a difficult topic. A woman I know, whose daughter had recently divorced, said to me, "She has broken a huge commandment of God, and I am so distressed by the punishment that will come to her!" This is not how I understand God. The way God seems to work is that he gives out numerous warnings about the paths that will lead us to unnecessary suffering. For instance: don't kill people, don't perjure, don't commit adultery, don't covet. He knows how he made us, and he knows what will hurt us and the people nearby. I think divorce falls in the same category. God is pleading "Love, love, love!" He is not waiting to punish; he is trying to prevent heartache. We should not punish divorced people either.

Genesis 2:18–24
Psalm 128:1–2,3,4–5,6
Hebrews 2:9–11
Mark 10:2–16 or 10:2–12

Monday

OCTOBER 4

• ST. FRANCIS OF ASSISI •

"Which of these three, in your opinion,
was neighbor to the robbers' victim?"
He answered, "The one who treated him with mercy."
Jesus said to him, "Go and do likewise."
—LUKE 10:36–37

St. Francis of Assisi threw himself into this Scripture reading. He showed mercy to everyone and was declared a great saint. The troubling part for me is that not everyone loved Francis in his own day. His father disowned him, the hierarchy of the church was not always on his side, and influential people in his town saw him as a threat to their way of life. Why does treating others with mercy often produce fear and anger in other people? I don't have an answer.

Jonah 1:1—2:1–2,11
Jonah 2:3,4,5,8
Luke 10:25–37

Tuesday

OCTOBER 5

• BLESSED FRANCIS XAVIER SEELOS, PRIEST •

Out of the depths I cry to you, O LORD;
LORD, hear my voice!
Let your ears be attentive
to my voice in supplication.
—PSALM 130:1B–2

Out of the depths of what? Sometimes, I cry out of the depths of my sins, asking for forgiveness. Other times, I cry out of the depths of despair, trying to swim to the surface. I have deep convictions that will make me cry out against the injustices in the world. But the best cry from the depths is when I feel that deep love and gratitude toward God and all he means to me.

Jonah 3:1–10
Psalm 130:1b–2,3–4ab,7–8
Luke 10:38–42

Wednesday

OCTOBER 6

• ST. BRUNO, PRIEST * BLESSED MARIE-ROSE DUROCHER, VIRGIN •

He said to them, "When you pray, say:

Father, hallowed be your name,
your Kingdom come.
Give us each day our daily bread
and forgive us our sins
for we ourselves forgive everyone in debt to us,
and do not subject us to the final test."
—LUKE 11:2–4

The Lord's Prayer is not necessarily words to memorize and repeat; it is a simple formula to practice. First, praise God and invite him to come. Ask for what you need today, not for tomorrow or the future—just today. We can ask for tomorrow's needs tomorrow. Ask for forgiveness and give forgiveness. And last of all: ask for God's protection from the pressures of the day.

Jonah 4:1–11
Psalm 86:3–4,5–6,9–10
Luke 11:1–4

"If you then, who are wicked,
know how to give good gifts to your children,
how much more will the Father in heaven
give the Holy Spirit
to those who ask him?"
—LUKE 11:13

I ask God to send his Spirit especially when I am feeling uncertain, unprepared, weak, or afraid. And God sends the Holy Spirit, but I am rarely aware of it in the moment. Once, after I gave a talk about St. Vincent de Paul in a ravaged neighborhood of Detroit, a lady came to me and said, "You have the Holy Spirit." I stared at her in astonishment and asked, "What is the Holy Spirit? I don't know why you are saying that." Equally astonished, she took my hand and said emphatically, "You have the Holy Spirit. Believe it." I know the bewilderment stayed on my face because she smiled encouragingly and patted my hand before she left.

Malachi 3:13–20b
Psalm 1:1–2,3,4 and 6
Luke 11:5–13

Let all who dwell in the land tremble,
for the day of the LORD is coming;
Yes, it is near, a day of darkness and of gloom,
a day of clouds and somberness!
—JOEL 2:1B–2

I don't, by preference, reflect on gloomy passages like this one from the prophet Joel, but since it has arrived today, let us ponder it. I know that God does not want us to be afraid—that admonishment is repeated over and over again in Scripture. I also know that God does not want us to be preoccupied with predicting the future. God prefers that we live in the present and put aside our tendency to scheme and overplan. A good father does not make a habit of frightening his children. Perhaps this passage is meant to counteract complacency? Maybe it is an exaggerated way of saying, "Stay awake!"

Joel 1:13–15; 2:1–2
Psalm 9:2–3,6 and 16,8–9
Luke 11:15–26

While Jesus was speaking,
a woman from the crowd called out and said to him,
"Blessed is the womb that carried you
and the breasts at which you nursed."
He replied, "Rather, blessed are those
who hear the word of God and observe it."
—LUKE 11:27–28

One would think that the Virgin Mary, mother of our Lord,
is the most blessed person in the history of humanity, but
Jesus says otherwise. You and I are blessed merely because we
listen to God's word and put it into practice. We are blessed
even if God does not ask martyrdom from us. We are blessed
even if God does not bestow on us miraculous powers. We
are blessed even if we live in a time when it is a struggle to be
good. Let's talk about being blessed a little more tomorrow.

Joel 4:12–21
Psalm 97:1–2,5–6,11–12
Luke 11:27–28

I prayed, and prudence was given me;
I pleaded, and the spirit of wisdom came to me.
—WISDOM 7:7

Solomon asked the Lord for wisdom above all blessings, and
the Lord granted his request. Was Solomon's life perfect or
worry-free? No. He was wise, but that did not make life
perfect. I have always sought understanding as well. It
seemed to me that if I could understand a situation, a person,
or my own heart, then I would be able to fix the problems
that appeared. But now, I am beginning to understand that
understanding is not the entire answer. Yesterday Jesus said,
"Rather, blessed are those who hear the word of God and
observe it." He didn't say we are blessed if we understand.
We are blessed if we obey. Am I advocating blind obedience?
No. *Guided* obedience—guided by the word and spirit of
God. More on obedience tomorrow.

Wisdom 7:7–11
Psalm 90:12–13,14–15,16–17(14)
Hebrews 4:12–13
Mark 10:17–30 or 10:17–27

OCTOBER 11

Through him we have received the grace of apostleship,
to bring about the obedience of faith,
for the sake of his name, among all the Gentiles,
among whom are you also, who are called
to belong to Jesus Christ;
—ROMANS 1:5–6

"The obedience of faith." For years, I practiced all the rules of the Catholic Church, even those that made no sense to me. My thinking was that if I agreed with all the rules, then what merit was there in obeying them? It was still me doing my own will. So, I obeyed the things that I *disagreed with* as a practice in spiritual humility. It was a good practice, and I don't regret it. Along the way I began to understand that *I* am the Catholic Church and that the spirit of God resides within me. Now, in some circumstances, I disobey some rules, which is *even more* spiritually humiliating.

Romans 1:1–7
Psalm 98:1,2–3ab,3cd–4
Luke 11:29–32

*The Pharisee was amazed to see
that he [Jesus] did not observe the prescribed washing
before the meal.*
—LUKE 11:38

Jesus is teaching the Pharisee that charity comes before rules.
In the St. Vincent de Paul Society, we are taught to recognize
the "hidden rules" of different economic classes. An example
of a middle-class hidden rule is that we pay our bills first
before we give money away. People living in poverty,
surrounded by others who are struggling, have a hidden rule
that says, first, take care of people's basic needs. My
coworker in this situation, before paying her own bills,
always gave a large portion of her paycheck to her
grandmother. Grandmother divided the money up among
the family members who were most in need. Why? Because
they knew that wealth is fleeting, and anyone could be in
need at any time. Now, read Luke 11:41.

Romans 1:16–25
Psalm 19:2–3,4–5
Luke 11:37–41

OCTOBER 13

Only in God is my soul at rest;
from him comes my salvation.
He only is my rock and my salvation,
my stronghold; I shall not be disturbed at all.
—PSALM 62:2–3

When I am feeling under pressure, taking on too many projects, and not sleeping well, Psalm 62 gathers me in. I repeat the words to myself and take a few minutes to sit still with God. But rest does not come from sitting. It does not come from going to bed, either. Rest comes only when my brain stops whirling, and that happens when I turn to God and give him my plans, my resentments, my pride, and my defenses. Giving up these makes room for God, and then I can rest. Stopping to rest is not defeat; it is a sign of victory over myself.

Romans 2:1–11
Psalm 62:2–3,6–7,9
Luke 11:42–46

Thursday

OCTOBER 14

• ST. CALLISTUS I, POPE AND MARTYR •

What occasion is there then for boasting? It is ruled out.
On what principle, that of works?
No, rather on the principle of faith.
For we consider that a person is justified by faith
apart from works of the law.
—ROMANS 3:27–28

Nonbelievers sometimes accuse religious people of being self-righteous. We are considered to be judgmental. It is feared that we are attempting to control other people in society through creating laws for everyone that adhere to our standards of good and evil. I agree with Paul when he writes, "What occasion is there then for boasting?" Our faith forbids us to boast of the good things we do. We surely may not boast of all the good things we attempt to make other people do either. We may only trust that our faith is true and hope it will keep us from trespassing against others. We have no occasion for boasting.

Romans 3:21–30
Psalm 130:1b–2,3–4,5–6ab
Luke 11:47–54

A worker's wage is credited not as a gift,
but as something due.
But when one does not work,
yet believes in the one who justifies the ungodly,
his faith is credited as righteousness.
—ROMANS 4:4–5

Paul is writing again about faith versus works. It was one of the loudest protests of the Protestant Reformation. Martin Luther insisted that no one is saved because of what he or she accomplishes but, rather, we are saved because of our faith given by God through mercy and grace. Many of the greatest Catholic saints taught the same thing. Teresa of Ávila did many good works (mostly reforming her order of nuns), but it was her faith that made her a Doctor of the Church.

Romans 4:1–8
Psalm 32:1b–2,5,11
Luke 12:1–7

"When they take you before synagogues and before
rulers and authorities,
do not worry about how or what your defense will be
or about what you are to say.
For the Holy Spirit will teach you at that moment
what you should say."
—LUKE 12:11–12

Does anyone else do this? I have a deep flaw: I need to have an excuse or argument ready in case anyone accuses me of neglect of duties, heresy, or arriving late. While my brain is busily explaining my action or inaction, it dawns on me that when my soul is filled to the brim with defenses, there is no room for the Holy Spirit. On a good day, I cease my inner arguments, take a deep breath, and repeat the name of Jesus until I tamp down my defensiveness.

Romans 4:13,16–18
Psalm 105:6–7,8–9,42–43
Luke 12:8–12

Sunday

OCTOBER 17

• TWENTY-NINTH SUNDAY IN ORDINARY TIME •

Because of his affliction
he shall see the light in fullness of days;
through his suffering, my servant shall justify many,
and their guilt he shall bear.
—ISAIAH 53:11

The suffering servant in Isaiah is beloved by God, but he suffers. Lack of suffering is not something to brag about, or to try to attain. Our faith is built on the image of the God who suffers, whose servants suffer, and whose beloved suffer. We are called to love God and love our neighbor; suffering is frequently part of that.

Isaiah 53:10–11
Psalm 33:4–5,18–19,20,22(22)
Hebrews 4:14–16
Mark 10:35–45 or 10:42–45

"Into whatever house you enter,
first say, 'Peace to this household.'
If a peaceful person lives there,
your peace will rest on him;
but if not, it will return to you.
Stay in the same house and eat and drink
what is offered to you,
for the laborer deserves payment.
Do not move about from one house to another.
Whatever town you enter and they welcome you,
eat what is set before you,
cure the sick in it and say to them,
'The Kingdom of God is at hand for you.'"
—LUKE 10:5–9

I chose a long passage from Luke's Gospel because it sums up what we are to do if we want to be disciples, evangelists, or merely workers in the field: visit people; bless them with our peace; eat with them; stay where we are welcome; cure the sick; tell them about God's presence. Simplicity itself.

2 Timothy 4:10–17b
Psalm 145:10–11,12–13,17–18
Luke 10:1–9

• ST. JOHN DE BRÉBEUF AND ST. ISAAC JOGUES, PRIESTS, AND
COMPANIONS, MARTYRS •

Sacrifice or oblation you wished not,
but ears open to obedience you gave me.
Burnt offerings or sin-offerings you sought not;
then said I, "Behold I come."
—PSALM 40:7–8A

God wants us to come to him. I suppose, if he wished, he
could appear before us and knock us to the ground as he did
St. Paul, but that doesn't seem to be his usual method.
Instead, he prefers that we come to him. He will not do
violence to our freedom. When we decide to approach the
Maker, the Source, the Love, the Peace, and the Mercy, we
need to be still, clear out other desires, and wait peacefully.
One more thing: God's presence is subtle when we are sitting
and waiting; later, as we are going about our day, his power
appears. But the coming and waiting part is crucial.

Romans 5:12,15b,17–19,20b–21
Psalm 40:7–8a,8b–9,10,17
Luke 12:35–38

*"Much will be required of the person
entrusted with much,
and still more will be demanded of the person
entrusted with more."*
—LUKE 12:48B

This is fair, right? If someone has a lot of money, then they should be expected to pay more taxes in support of the community where the money came from. If someone has only a little money, then they pay the community a little money back. This is common sense. And, according to Jesus, this idea works in the spiritual life. If I have been given the chance to receive God's forgiveness, joy, faith, or love, then absolutely, it is my responsibility to share them. If you have received very little from God, then God will not expect you to share much. This may be a good day to take an inventory to figure out where you stand.

Romans 6:12–18
Psalm 124:1b–3,4–6,7–8
Luke 12:39–48

OCTOBER 21

*Blessed the man who follows not
the counsel of the wicked
Nor walks in the way of sinners,
nor sits in the company of the insolent.*
—PSALM 1:1

A decade ago, we lent our television to someone who needed
a small set for their bedroom while they were convalescing.
Unexpectedly, we were happier without it. It's not like we
were cut off from the world; we still had access to news,
sports, and entertainment from our computers. But we no
longer found it acceptable to "sit in the company of the
insolent." Through television, even when a character was not
the type of person we would invite into our home, out of
habit, curiosity, or laziness, we allowed that character in. I
now notice the obnoxious behavior of people who sit in my
living room through media, and I delete them.

Romans 6:19–23
Psalm 1:1–2,3,4 and 6
Luke 12:49–53

Friday

OCTOBER 22

• ST. JOHN PAUL II, POPE •

For I do not do the good I want,
but I do the evil I do not want.
—ROMANS 7:19

Anyone who has ever been on a restricted diet knows the contrariness of our own natures.

We want to eat the right food because of the benefits, but then we see something as unappealing as a vending machine, and all our power of resistance disappears. Why are we this way? Original sin? Egoism? The devil? It doesn't matter so much how we explain our sin; it matters that we recognize our helplessness, which is what Paul is saying in this passage: We need God's help. So, let's ask for it.

Romans 7:18–25a
Psalm 119:66,68,76,77,93,94
Luke 12:54–59

*"Or those eighteen people who were killed
when the tower at Siloam fell on them—
do you think they were more guilty
than everyone else who lives in Jerusalem?
By no means!
But I tell you, if you do not repent,
you will all perish as they did!"*
—LUKE 13:4–5

Jesus lays to rest the notion that people who suffer do so because they are more sinful than other people who do not suffer as much. Not so. Don't let your mind go in this direction, because it is simply not true. So, how shall we view people who are suffering excessively? "There, but for the grace of God, go I." What shall we make of "if you do not repent, you will all perish"? Again, no one is more or less guilty than anyone else. So, repent, and be saved. Everyone sins, and everyone can be saved.

Romans 8:1–11
Psalm 24:1b–2,3–4ab,5–6
Luke 13:1–9

Sunday

OCTOBER 24

· THIRTIETH SUNDAY IN ORDINARY TIME · ·

Jesus stopped and said, "Call him."
So they called the blind man, saying to him,
"Take courage; get up, Jesus is calling you."
—MARK 10:49

Whatever it is inside of you that holds you down, whatever depresses you, or whatever you have been praying about for a long time, "Take courage; get up, Jesus is calling you."

Jeremiah 31:7–9
Psalm 126:1–2,2–3,4–5,6(3)
Hebrews 5:1–6
Mark 10:46–52

OCTOBER 25

Blessed day by day be the LORD,
who bears our burdens; God, who is our salvation.
God is a saving God for us;
the LORD, my Lord, controls the passageways of death.
—PSALM 68:20–21

There was a day when the burden of someone else's sin was weighing heavily on me. A young mother I met at the St. Vincent de Paul thrift store gave me some of the best advice I ever received from anyone. She looked calmly at me and held up three fingers. "Three things to remember," she said. "Pray about it first. Then, release it—give it over to God. And lastly—and this is important, so pay attention—don't try to save that person. God saves people, you don't."

Romans 8:12–17
Psalm 68:2 and 4,6–7ab,20,21
Luke 13:10–17

OCTOBER 26

For in hope we were saved.
Now hope that sees for itself is not hope.
For who hopes for what one sees?
But if we hope for what we do not see, we wait
with endurance.
—ROMANS 8:24–25

When the road is uphill or in a dark wood, I begin to pine for
assistance, a different path, or a miracle. This type of hope is
what I call "rescue hope." It differs from "the next thing on
my bucket list" kind of hope. Meeting people in poverty
opened my eyes to these two kinds of hope. Sometime, make
a list of your hopes, then split the list into "rescue" and
"bucket list." The bucket list hopes are not the kind that
save us.

Romans 8:18–25
Psalm 126:1b–2ab,2cd–3,4–5,6
Luke 13:18–21

OCTOBER 27

The Spirit comes to the aid of our weakness,
for we do not know how to pray as we ought,
but the Spirit himself intercedes with
inexpressible groanings.
—ROMANS 8:26

After my years of praying, this verse strikes my heart. It's true that I "do not know how to pray as we ought." If prayer is a conversation with God, I still monopolize the conversation with my many words and barely give God space to utter a simple thought or piece of advice. Poor God! I picture God hanging out, hoping to get a word in edgewise, and all the while I am chattering about this or that or nothing at all.

Thank goodness that, at times, weakness, silence, and weariness overwhelm me, and the Spirit can intercede.

Romans 8:26–30
Psalm 13:4–5,6
Luke 13:22–30

OCTOBER 28

Brothers and sisters:
You are no longer strangers and sojourners,
but you are fellow citizens with the holy ones
and members of the household of God,
built upon the foundation of the Apostles
and prophets,
with Christ Jesus himself as the capstone.
—EPHESIANS 2:19–20

One day as my husband and I were driving home from Chicago through the South Side, Dean pointed out that we were passing the National Shrine of St. Jude. "Can we stop?" I asked. "We can try," he said, "but I doubt it's open. This is a rough neighborhood." The church was surrounded by decaying structures and battered streets but was unlocked. I went in, lit a candle for my friend recently diagnosed with cancer, and thanked St. Jude, patron of hopeless cases. That was five years ago, and my friend is in remission. *We are no longer strangers and sojourners.*

Ephesians 2:19–22
Psalm 19:2–3,4–5
Luke 6:12–16

Friday

OCTOBER 29

In front of him there was a man suffering from dropsy.
Jesus spoke to the scholars of the law and the Pharisees
in reply, asking,
"Is it lawful to cure on the sabbath or not?"
But they kept silent; so he took the man and,
after he had healed him, dismissed him.
—LUKE 14:2–4

Wouldn't it be a mess if the sick, the poor, and all kinds of
desperate people showed up every Sunday at Mass and
waited in the back of church for us to pray over them and
heal them, and then put their hands out for assistance? Can
you imagine walking through crowds of needy people right
after receiving communion?

Actually . . . I wonder why they aren't there in hoards?

Romans 9:1–5
Psalm 147:12–13,14–15,19–20
Luke 14:1–6

OCTOBER 30

The LORD will not cast off his people.
—PSALM 94:14A

The Lord will not abandon me, but I can very quickly abandon the Lord. If I throw myself into solving crises or intimidating opponents or folding into defeat, then I am abandoning God's love and care. So, I try to remember whenever I am at a loss, when I don't know what direction to take, when words fail me or no one seems trustworthy, that such a time is when the Lord becomes my refuge. I sit still, close my eyes, and try to evict the fears, resentments, and defenses that my smallness constructs. None of those feelings is based in reality. I remind myself that I have nothing to fear, that I am the heir of the King, and that he counts every hair on my head. I say, "Jesus" over and over again, slowly. God will not abandon me; I must not abandon God.

Romans 11:1–2a,11–12,25–29
Psalm 94:12–13a,14–15,17–18
Luke 14:1,7–11

OCTOBER 31

• THIRTY-FIRST SUNDAY IN ORDINARY TIME •

One of the scribes came to Jesus and asked him,
"Which is the first of all the commandments?"
—MARK 12:28B

The scribe had an opportunity to ask Jesus a question, and he
asked a good one, although it sounds in the story as if he
already knew the answer. No matter. Perhaps he wanted to
verify that Jesus knew theology—he was a scribe, after all. If
today you were given the chance to stand in front of Jesus
and ask him one question, what would it be? Think about
this seriously for a few minutes. Close your eyes. Picture
Jesus sitting on a large stone, resting, unhurried, waiting to
hear your question. His mild eyes are gazing at you curiously,
a slight smile of encouragement on his lips. What question
comes to your mind?

Deuteronomy 6:2–6
Psalm 18:2–3,3–4,47,51(2)
Hebrews 7:23–28
Mark 12:28b–34

NOVEMBER 1

Then one of the elders spoke up and said to me,
"Who are these wearing white robes,
and where did they come from?"
I said to him, "My lord, you are the one who knows."
He said to me,
"These are the ones who have survived
the time of great distress;
they have washed their robes
and made them white in the Blood of the Lamb."
—REVELATION 7:13–14

Have you ever worn a white robe? I wore one for graduation.
Because of the translucent, stiff material, the formal effect is
ruined by the wrong clothing underneath. Our advisor told us
that under no circumstances could we wear red, black, or any
loudly patterned dresses under the robes. "Keep it simple,
neutral, and approximately knee length," she advised. When
we get our white robes, it is wise to remember that anything
brash will probably show through.

Revelation 7:2–4,9–14   1 John 3:1–3
Psalm 24:1b–2,3–4ab,5–6   Matthew 5:1–12a

NOVEMBER 2

"For this is the will of my Father,
that everyone who sees the Son and believes in him
may have eternal life,
and I shall raise him on the last day."
—JOHN 6:40

I picture myself dying suddenly and now I am standing in
line, waiting my turn with everyone else who died the instant
I did. The person I have avoided for the past ten years just
happens to be behind me in line. I am perfectly safe: angels
line the pathway. I have a choice: turn around, acknowledge
this person with a handshake of peace and forgiveness, or
continue facing forward. Try this yourself. Choose now.
Next, picture the two of you approaching Jesus. What kind
of look does he have on his face when he sees the two of you
coming toward him?

Wisdom 3:1–9
Psalm 23:1–3,4,5,6
Romans 5:5–11 or 6:3–9
John 6:37–40
Other readings may be chosen.

NOVEMBER 3

• ST. MARTIN DE PORRES, RELIGIOUS •

Brothers and sisters:
Owe nothing to anyone, except to love one another;
for the one who loves another has fulfilled the law.
—ROMANS 13:8

Wait a second. What if, as the author of Romans writes, we
owe it to people to love them?

Romans 13:8–10
Psalm 112:1b–2,4–5,9
Luke 14:25–33

Wait for the LORD with courage;
be stouthearted, and wait for the LORD.
—PSALM 27:14

Who waits? Pregnant women wait nine months, much of that
time uncomfortably. People who have had a medical test
done sometimes wait for days in anxiety. Travelers wait in
traffic jams. Poor people wait a lot. They wait for necessities
to go on sale, for decisions by social-service agencies, in
emergency rooms, at bus stops, in food lines, for subsidized
housing to open up, between split shifts, and on park
benches. They are the queens and kings of waiting. And, in
my experience, they spend much of this waiting in prayer.
They truly wait for the Lord.

Romans 14:7–12
Psalm 27:1bcde,4,13–14
Luke 15:1–10

*"And the master commended that dishonest steward
for acting prudently.
For the children of this world
are more prudent in dealing with their own generation
than the children of light."*
—LUKE 16:8

A man who was convinced of the truth of the Gospel
cornered me at a conference and attempted to "convict" me.
He repeatedly used the word *convict*, insisting that a person
could not be saved until she acknowledged her own
sinfulness and turned to the Lord in abject humility. I wasn't
opposed to what he was saying, but the way he was telling
me all this with finger pointed at me and voice above
conversation level, I was thinking only of a polite way to
escape from him. Jesus holds up the dishonest servant as a
smart way to convert people to our side: *write off their debts*.
They will convict themselves when they are ready; that's not
our job.

Romans 15:14–21
Psalm 98:1,2–3ab,3cd–4
Luke 16:1–8

Jesus said to his disciples: "I tell you, make friends for yourselves with dishonest wealth, so that when it fails, you will be welcomed into eternal dwellings."

—LUKE 16:9

In a continuation of yesterday's passage about the dishonest steward, a couple of things stand out: Jesus assumes that we all have dishonest wealth and that it will fail. What is this dishonest wealth? Did you come upon your health honestly through a wholesome diet, regular check-ups, and abstinence from stimulants? Or, perhaps, have you overeaten unhealthy things and failed to exercise regularly? Then your good health may be dishonest wealth. Do you have an education that no one outside of your family subsidized? Meaning no public schools, no parish-subsidized Catholic school, no school volunteers, no outside donors to fundraisers, or grossly underpaid staff. If so, your education is also dishonest wealth. Do good with wealth now because Jesus warns that it will eventually fail.

Romans 16:3–9,16,22–27
Psalm 145:2–3,4–5,10–11
Luke 16:9–15

Sunday

NOVEMBER 7

· THIRTY-SECOND SUNDAY IN ORDINARY TIME ·

She left and did as Elijah had said.
She was able to eat for a year, and he and her son as well;
the jar of flour did not go empty,
nor the jug of oil run dry,
as the LORD had foretold through Elijah.
—1 KINGS 17:15–16

Like the widow, sometimes I worry about things running dry or going empty. Our retirement is in the stock market, and when it fluctuates, I feel uneasy. If farmers have a bad year and food prices rise, I get anxious. But God says, "Peace be with you" and "Be not afraid." I can believe that God is trustworthy because I believe that I am not seeing everything that is. This world is only a small part of what God has created, and I am only a tiny bit of what God is. I am a speck in his heart. And he loves that speck.

1 Kings 17:10–16
Psalm 146:7,8–9,9–10(1b)
Hebrews 9:24–28
Mark 12:38–44 or 12:41–44

⋺344⋲

*Because he is found by those who test him not,
and he manifests himself to those who do not
disbelieve him.*
—WISDOM 1:2

Whether a person is born and raised in a church community or converts later in life, there is a moment for each of us when we must ask ourselves, *I wonder if it's all true?* It is a disturbing moment, and as St. Vincent de Paul says, "We must be willing to be disturbed." *I won't believe unless I see the marks of the nails in his hands* is a different thing than *could it possibly all be true?* The former is more like folding our arms, refusing to look around, and saying, "Prove it." The latter statement finds us on the brink of the cliff, peering over the edge. The former "tests him," and the latter does "not disbelieve him."

Wisdom 1:1–7
Psalm 139:1b–3,4–6,7–8,9–10
Luke 17:1–6

He [Jesus] made a whip out of cords
and drove them all out of the temple area,
with the sheep and oxen,
and spilled the coins of the money-changers
and overturned their tables,
and to those who sold doves he said,
"Take these out of here,
and stop making my Father's house a marketplace."
—JOHN 2:15–16

Brothers and sisters:
You are God's building.
—1 CORINTHIANS 3:9C

Put these two passages together, and perhaps we get this:
Jesus made a whip of cords and drove out all of you, and
spilled your money, and overturned your props, and said,
"Take the creatures out of here and stop marketing yourself."

Ezekiel 47:1–2,8–9,12
Psalm 46:2–3,5–6,8–9
1 Corinthians 3:9c–11,16–17
John 2:13–22

*For the lowly may be pardoned out of mercy
but the mighty shall be mightily put to the test.*
—WISDOM 6:6

One of the startling things I learned working with people in
poverty is that few of them think of themselves as needy.
Often I hear them say, "I'm just going through a rough patch"
or "There's a lot of people worse off than me" or even "I don't
like to take food away from somebody at the pantry who
really needs it." Poor people rarely identify as poor.
Conversely, other times I have heard well-off people identify
as poor: "Who do you think is going to pay for this?" or
"Money doesn't grow on trees" or "Good help is hard to
come by these days." Often, the lowly aren't even aware that
they are lowly, and the mighty are much the same.

Wisdom 6:1–11
Psalm 82:3–4,6–7
Luke 17:11–19

> *Jesus said in reply,*
> *"The coming of the Kingdom of God*
> *cannot be observed,*
> *and no one will announce, 'Look, here it is,' or,*
> *'There it is.'*
> *For behold, the Kingdom of God is among you."*
> —LUKE 17:20B–21

The kingdom of God is among us. Does Jesus mean the church? I doubt it, because it is split into factions, and God wouldn't allow his kingdom to be splintered up like that. Does he mean nature? Perhaps partially, but he also says that the kingdom cannot be observed, so nature is not the complete presence of God's kingdom because it is very observable. The kingdom cannot be observed, no one will see it coming, and it is already among us. That sounds like the definition of love to me.

Wisdom 7:22b—8:1
Psalm 119:89,90,91,130,135,175
Luke 17:20–25

But yet, for these the blame is less;
For they indeed have gone astray perhaps,
though they seek God and wish to find him.
For they search busily among his works,
but are distracted by what they see,
because the things seen are fair.
—WISDOM 13:6–7

I am not the only person on the planet who is seeking God.
You are, as well, or you wouldn't be reading this book. People
seek God by reading, through prayer, in fellowship with
other God seekers, by observing nature, and by serving
others. We seek God through worship, through music, and
through praise. Some of us seek God by quieting our minds,
sitting still, emptying our ego, and listening. And each of us
God seekers is "distracted" in one way or another. The world
and ourselves are big distractions, yet it is in them that we
find God. Oh, how God loves paradoxes!

Wisdom 13:1–9
Psalm 19:2–3,4–5ab
Luke 17:26–37

*"But when the Son of Man comes, will he find
faith on earth?"*
—LUKE 18:8

Just before asking this rhetorical question, Jesus has told the disciples a parable about persevering in prayer. Then he asks if there will be faith on earth when he comes. He doesn't ask if the churches or synagogues will be full. He doesn't ask if all the laws in the land will follow Christian doctrine. He doesn't ask if there will be numerous vocations to the religious life. He doesn't ask if all the sexual sins will have been erased. He doesn't even ask if charity will overflow or if peace will reign. He is wondering if people will be persisting in prayer. Keep praying, keep talking to God, because he will not be looking for his stewards, his employees, his officials, or his sinless, long-faced devotees. He will be looking for the friends who converse with him every day.

Wisdom 18:14–16; 19:6–9
Psalm 105:2–3,36–37,42–43
Luke 18:1–8

NOVEMBER 14

• THIRTY-THIRD SUNDAY IN ORDINARY TIME •

"At that time there shall arise
Michael, the great prince,
guardian of your people;
it shall be a time unsurpassed in distress
since nations began until that time.
At that time your people shall escape,
everyone who is found written in the book."
—DANIEL 12:1

Well, we can't say we haven't been warned. The trouble with
prophecies and warnings is that we don't want to believe
them. We want to believe that everything is fine, that there is
no reason to get excited, and that even if things turn sour, we
ourselves will not be crushed. Let's reflect, not on the
Apocalypse but on this strange desire to believe in salvation.
Where does it come from, this lack of despair? Why is denial
of disaster considered delusional? Could it be that in our
innermost being we know that God holds us and will never
let us go?

Daniel 12:1–3
Psalm 16:5,8,9–10,11(1)
Hebrews 10:11–14,18
Mark 13:24–32

> *He shouted, "Jesus, Son of David, have pity on me!"*
> *The people walking in front rebuked him,*
> *telling him to be silent,*
> *but he kept calling out all the more,*
> *"Son of David, have pity on me!"*
> —LUKE 18:38–39

Jesus was well known as a healer. How odd that the people walking in front of Jesus' entourage rebuked the blind beggar and told him to be silent. Jesus, of course, heard the man's cries and quickly cured him. This passage warns me about two things. First, being at the head of the procession does not make one an expert, or even very wise. Second, if someone who is at the head of the procession tells me to stop speaking up, that is not necessarily what Jesus wants.

1 Maccabees 1:10–15,41–43,54–57,62–63
Psalm 119:53,61,134,150,155,158
Luke 18:35–43

NOVEMBER 16

At that time Jesus came to Jericho and intended to
pass through the town. . . .
Jesus looked up and said,
"Zacchaeus, come down quickly,
for today I must stay at your house."
—LUKE 19:1,5B

Jesus' plans are interruptible. He was intending to pass through Jericho, but when he saw the sinner Zacchaeus in the tree, the trip was brought to a halt and Jesus stayed that night instead. Remember this story if you ever worry that God can't be persuaded. God will stop and help anyone who is looking for him. God will even change his plans to save that person.

2 Maccabees 6:18–31
Psalm 3:2–3,4–5,6–7
Luke 19:1–10

"Son, have pity on me, who carried you in my
womb for nine months,
nursed you for three years, brought you up,
educated and supported you to your present age.
I beg you, child, to look at the heavens and the earth
and see all that is in them;
then you will know that God did not make them
out of existing things;
and in the same way the human race came
into existence."
—2 MACCABEES 7:22–23

This mother does not claim her sons as her own. She gives
the whole story of how she was pregnant, then nursed,
educated, and supported them, yet she does not claim their
undying devotion. She points to God as the One who
created them and who deserves their loyalty. This is a
particular reminder to me today because it is my birthday.

2 Maccabees 7:1,20–31
Psalm 17:1bcd,5–6,8b and 15
Luke 19:11–28

• THE DEDICATION OF THE BASILICA OF ST. PETER AND ST. PAUL, APOSTLES
* ST. ROSE PHILIPPINE DUCHESNE, VIRGIN •

> *"They will smash you to the ground*
> *and your children within you,*
> *and they will not leave one stone upon another*
> *within you*
> *because you did not recognize the time*
> *of your visitation."*
> —LUKE 19:44

Jesus is lamenting over Jerusalem, but he could also be lamenting over any soul. I wonder, does everyone have a visitation from God? Jesus speaks of "the time of your visitation," not of "a visitation." He seems to imply that there is a time for each of us to be visited. The Bible backs this idea with the stories of Adam, Noah, Abraham, Isaac, Jacob, Moses, David, Mary and Joseph, Andrew and John, Peter and Paul. It seems that the time of visitation is a constant, and perhaps that is why these stories are in the Holy Scriptures. Do you recognize a time when you were visited by emissaries from the other side of the veil?

1 Maccabees 2:15–29 or Acts 28:11–16,30–31
Psalm 50:1b–2,5–6,14–15 or 98:1,2–3ab,3cd–4,5–6
Luke 19:41–44 or Matthew 14:22–33

And every day he was teaching in the temple area.
The chief priests, the scribes, and the leaders
of the people, meanwhile,
were seeking to put him to death,
—LUKE 19:47

At this point in the story of Jesus' ministry, it is late and the Passion and Crucifixion are close. Jesus knows this, of course. He has often spoken of "his time" and has shown an ability to read people's hearts. So, what does he do when he knows that time is short? He teaches in the very place where his enemies gather to plot his capture and death. Perhaps he is still hoping that he can reach a few of his misguided enemies, pull them away from jealousy, anger, greed, disbelief, and fear. He hasn't given up on them even as they plan how to get rid of him. He hasn't given up on us, either.

1 Maccabees 4:3–37,52–59
1 Chronicles 29:10bcd,11abc,11d–12a,12bcd
Luke 19:45–48

NOVEMBER 20

Some of the scribes said in reply,
"Teacher, you have answered well."
And they no longer dared to ask him anything.
—LUKE 20:39–40

How strange is this? The scribes admit that Jesus answered
the question well, and then they no longer ask him any more
questions! When I applied to go to college, the school
administered a placement test in writing and math. The
results were mixed: I did well on the writing test and
mediocre in math. The school waived the usual requirement
for a writing class and advised me to take more math. I ended
up majoring in math, struggling all four years. How strange is
this? In writing, when I answered the questions well, I was
advised to stop there. Do we do this in the spiritual life as
well? If someone says they converse with God, do we no
longer dare to ask them anything?

1 Maccabees 6:1–13
Psalm 9:2–3,4 and 6,16 and 19
Luke 20:27–40

Behold, he is coming amid the clouds,
and every eye will see him,
even those who pierced him.
All the peoples of the earth will lament him.
Yes. Amen.
—REVELATION 1:7

He is "amid the clouds," yet everyone will see him. Have you ever been in an airplane amid the clouds? All that can be seen are clouds. We have to trust that the earth is still below us. Our king, Jesus, has always abided amid the clouds. Pilate asks him straight out, "Are you the King of the Jews?" Jesus gives him a cloudy answer: "Do you say this on your own, or have others told you about me?" Jesus remained in the clouds because Pilate had only secondhand questions. If we want to see Jesus despite the cloudiness of living on earth, then we must ask the question on our own: *Jesus, are you my king?*

Daniel 7:13–14
Psalm 93:1,1–2,5(1a)
Revelation 1:5–8
John 18:33b–37

Glory and praise forever!
—DANIEL 3:52B

One time when Dean and I were on vacation, I asked him where he wanted to go to church on Sunday morning. He answered, "Any church is fine, except I don't feel up to a lot of praise music." I had to chuckle, because Dean loves church music and liturgy, but sometimes it's just not a day for amplifiers. I'm not criticizing church musicians. I love church music too, and this is the feast of St. Cecilia, patron of sacred music. I do wonder why I don't always feel like loudly praising God. He is the creator, the great giver, the source of all love, and of all there is—I should want to sing praises every minute. But sometimes, I just want to sit quietly in his presence and bask in his love. Perhaps that is the glory part?

Daniel 1:1–6,8–20
Daniel 3:52,53,54,55,56
Luke 21:1–4

• ST. CLEMENT I, POPE AND MARTYR • ST. COLUMBAN, ABBOT • BLESSED
MIGUEL AUGUSTÍN PRO, PRIEST AND MARTYR •

He [Jesus] answered,
"See that you not be deceived,
for many will come in my name, saying,
'I am he,' and 'The time has come.'
Do not follow them!"
—LUKE 21:8

Do you remember how John the Baptist came announcing
that everyone should repent and get ready for the Messiah?
He never claimed to be the Messiah himself but only the
precursor. "I am not worthy to loosen the thongs of his
sandals," he said. And when Jesus began his ministry, John
said, "He must increase, and I must decrease." Humility is a
trait of a true prophet. I think Jesus may be telling us that in
confusing times it's best to follow the humble.

Daniel 2:31–45
Daniel 3:57,58,59,60,61
Luke 21:5–11

Jesus said to the crowd:
"They will seize and persecute you. . . .
It will lead to your giving testimony."
—LUKE 21:12B,13

I pay attention to the God followers who are being seized
and persecuted. Their testimony has authority because they
are paying a price to give it. I'm suspicious, however, of the
ones who *claim* to be persecuted. They are rarely seized or
silenced, but they like to say that they are. Claiming to be
persecuted is quite different from *being* persecuted. It looks to
me like the people who most often complained that they
were being treated unfairly were the Pharisees and
the scribes.

Daniel 5:1–6,13–14,16–17,23–28
Daniel 3:62,63,64,65,66,67
Luke 21:12–19

NOVEMBER 25

• ST. CATHERINE OF ALEXANDRIA, VIRGIN AND MARTYR •
THANKSGIVING DAY •

*"There will be signs in the sun, the moon, and the stars,
and on earth nations will be in dismay,
perplexed by the roaring of the sea and the waves."*
—LUKE 21:25

These are clear signs. The sun, moon, and stars are generally
constant and predictable, so when these celestial entities
change or act differently, that is as good a sign as we could
ask for. But I doubt that the signs Jesus describes are meant to
tell us it's time to repent. It's pretty clear that repenting at the
last moment is not the kind of faith God is hoping to find in
us. It's true that God accepts deathbed confessions, but
why wait?

Daniel 6:12–28
Daniel 3:68,69,70,71,72,73,74
Luke 21:20–28
Mass in Thanksgiving to God:
Sirach 50:22–24
Psalm 138:1–2a,2bc–3,4–5
1 Corinthians 1:3–9
Luke 17:11–19
Other readings may be chosen.

NOVEMBER 26

*"Amen, I say to you, this generation will not pass away
until all these things have taken place.
Heaven and earth will pass away,
but my words will not pass away."*
—LUKE 21:32–33

If you are like me, you have heard plenty of explanations
about these verses and why Jesus seems to be talking about
the end of times and saying that it will happen before his
present generation ends. Obviously, this did not happen. I'm
not going to speculate on why. Passages like these say to me
that it is not simple to interpret Scripture, and anyone who
says that they know the meaning of a particular passage
probably knows only part of it. That's okay. We all "see
through a glass darkly," as Paul put it. All I have written in
these pages is only partial seeing, but your seeing added to
mine is bound to be better.

Daniel 7:2–14
Daniel 3:75,76,77,78,79,80,81
Luke 21:29–33

NOVEMBER 27

*"For that day will assault everyone
who lives on the face of the earth."*
—LUKE 21:35B

Everyone? This makes sense. Jesus doesn't want us to panic
over our individual or local misfortunes and disasters and
begin to fear it is the end of times. When the tribulations
come, they will affect everyone. We will know Jesus is
coming back when *everyone* is in trouble. Meanwhile, it is still
ordinary times, so when our neighbors are in trouble, we
ought to help them as much as we can. That commandment
has been in place for over two thousand years. Jesus never
told us to stockpile weapons and canned goods. He told us to
put up treasure in heaven.

Daniel 7:15–27
Daniel 3:82,83,84,85,86,87
Luke 21:34–36

NOVEMBER 28

• FIRST SUNDAY OF ADVENT •

May the Lord make you increase and abound in love
for one another and for all,
just as we have for you,
so as to strengthen your hearts,
to be blameless in holiness before our God and Father
at the coming of our Lord Jesus with all his holy ones.
Amen.

—1 THESSALONIANS 3:12–13

"Amen." This amen comes in the middle of the reading, and is such a beautiful place to pause and say, "Yes, amen." Dear reader, may the Lord make you increase and abound in love during this Advent season, so that when Christmas comes, you may be blameless in holiness. Amen!

Jeremiah 33:14–16
Psalm 25:4–5,8–9,10,14(1b)
1 Thessalonians 3:12—4:2
Luke 21:25–28,34–36

When Jesus heard this, he was amazed and said to
those following him,
"Amen, I say to you, in no one in Israel
have I found such faith.
I say to you, many will come from the east and the west,
and will recline with Abraham, Isaac, and Jacob
at the banquet in the Kingdom of heaven."

—MATTHEW 8:10–11

In the Society of St. Vincent de Paul, our primary contact with people in need is to visit their homes. We climb the steps they climb, sit on their chairs (or floors, if there are no chairs), and listen to their stories, as long as it takes. Then we attempt to assist them with the need they think is most pressing. After that, we pray with them, and often, I can say with Jesus, "Amen, in no one in the church have I found such faith." That's why they are my teachers.

Isaiah 2:1–5
Psalm 122:1–2,3–4b,4cd–5,6–7,8–9
Matthew 8:5–11

NOVEMBER 30

• ST. ANDREW, APOSTLE •

As Jesus was walking by the Sea of Galilee,
he saw two brothers,
Simon who is called Peter, and his brother Andrew,
casting a net into the sea; they were fishermen.
He said to them,
"Come after me, and I will make you fishers of men."
—MATTHEW 4:18–19

Notice that Andrew and Peter were not in the synagogue praying when Jesus called them. They were not assisting the needy, either. They were just busy with their usual daily work. I have a feeling that they were prayerful, generous men, but they had a job to do, and while they were doing that job, Jesus spoke to them. This story makes me content to go to work and to clean the house.

Romans 10:9–18
Psalm 19:8,9,10,11
Matthew 4:18–22

DECEMBER 1

Then he [Jesus] took the seven loaves and the fish,
gave thanks, broke the loaves,
and gave them to the disciples, who in turn
gave them to the crowds.
—MATTHEW 15:36

I might look at this story and say to myself, "Wow, it was miraculous of Jesus to feed the crowd." But, actually, the disciples were given the job of feeding the crowd. Jesus told the disciples that he pitied the hungry people. Next, he asked them how much food they had. Then he gave thanks for the meager supplies and told the disciples to distribute them. Jesus neither supplied the food nor distributed it—the disciples did both. Jesus *multiplied* the food. All we have to do is see God's pity, offer what we have, and give it away. It is not our job to save humanity. That is God's job. It is absolutely our job to share what we have.

Isaiah 25:6–10a
Psalm 23:1–3a,3b–4,5,6
Matthew 15:29–37

He humbles those in high places,
and the lofty city he brings down;
He tumbles it to the ground,
levels it with the dust.
It is trampled underfoot by the needy,
by the footsteps of the poor.
—ISAIAH 26:5–6

When my time comes to face Jesus, I pray that I will be
walking with the poor instead of looking down on them from
the high places, saying, "Lord, Lord."

Isaiah 26:1–6
Psalm 118:1 and 8–9,19–21,25–27a
Matthew 7:21,24–27

One thing I ask of the LORD;
this I seek:
To dwell in the house of the LORD
all the days of my life,
That I may gaze on the loveliness of the LORD
and contemplate his temple.
—PSALM 27:4

If God came to you and asked you to name one thing you would like him to do for you, would it be this? Me, neither. I would probably choose health or justice or freedom from anxiety. But I believe it is true that if I knew God well, then, without hesitating, being in his presence would be the one thing I would ask for. If I knew how much God loved me, if I trusted in his absolute mercy, if I believed him to be the source of every good thing, then, of course, I would be like the psalmist and ask to dwell in his presence.

Isaiah 29:17–24
Psalm 27:1,4,13–14
Matthew 9:27–31

DECEMBER 4

• ST. JOHN DAMASCENE, PRIEST AND DOCTOR OF THE CHURCH •

No longer will your Teacher hide himself,
but with your own eyes you shall see your Teacher,
While from behind, a voice shall sound in your ears:
"This is the way; walk in it."
—ISAIAH 30:20B–21A

My grandmother was a teacher, and my father was a teacher;
so were my aunt and my cousin. I was raised by teachers. For
me this verse is a lovely way to describe God: a teacher we
can see and whose voice gives clear instructions *from behind.* A
master teacher does not always stand in the front of the
room. She walks through the rows of desks and leans over
the students' shoulders, examining their work for praise or
pointing out corrections. If the class gets noisy, she stands up
and makes eye contact with everyone in the room. "Work
together quietly," she says. "Raise your hand if you have a
question." Sounds like God to me.

Isaiah 30:19–21,23–26
Psalm 147:1–2,3–4,5–6
Matthew 9:35—10:1,5a,6–8

DECEMBER 5

• SECOND SUNDAY OF ADVENT •

*I am confident of this,
that the one who began a good work in you
will continue to complete it
until the day of Christ Jesus.*
—PHILIPPIANS 1:6

What is this "good work" that Paul writes about? Once Jesus has us in his hand, he will not let us go. When we turn, in full awareness of our lowliness and of God's awesomeness, and we reach for Jesus' hand, he will not fail to grasp ours. He is waiting for us to move only a tiny centimeter in his direction. He doesn't want us to do a thing except say his name. We were put here to learn how to love God and neighbor. God is love. Reach out and receive. God will complete the work.

Baruch 5:1–9
Psalm 126:1–2,2–3,4–5,6(3)
Philippians 1:4–6,8–11
Luke 3:1–6

DECEMBER 6

• ST. NICHOLAS, BISHOP •

Then astonishment seized them all and they
glorified God,
and, struck with awe, they said,
"We have seen incredible things today."
—LUKE 5:26

The individual words in this verse make me shiver:
astonishment, seized, glorified, struck, awe, and *incredible.* All in one
sentence. This is the sort of feeling we try to create for our
young children at Christmastime. We love to see their
mouths drop open, their eyes light up, and their quivering
fingers fumbling with the ribbons. God is a parent like any
other parent. He delights in our astonished awe at his
incredible gifts. Go ahead and let yourself enjoy God's gifts
the way you want the gifts you bestow to be enjoyed. You
could not make God happier.

Isaiah 35:1–10
Psalm 85:9ab and 10,11–12,13–14
Luke 5:17–26

Comfort, give comfort to my people,
says your God.
Speak tenderly to Jerusalem, and proclaim to her
that her service is at an end,
her guilt is expiated;
Indeed, she has received from the hand of the LORD
double for all her sins.
—ISAIAH 40:1–2

These two verses alone are a good-enough reason to read the Bible. Don't we all need comfort? Are we not afraid that our sins will plague us forever? These verses from Isaiah say that God wants the prophet to speak comfort to his people and to tell them that the hard work is over. You can relax now. Open your tightly shut eyes and snuggle close to the God who loves and forgives you.

Isaiah 40:1–11
Psalm 96:1–2,3 and 10ac,11–12,13
Matthew 18:12–14

DECEMBER 8

• THE IMMACULATE CONCEPTION OF THE BLESSED VIRGIN MARY (PATRONAL
FEAST DAY OF THE UNITED STATES OF AMERICA) •

After the man, Adam, had eaten of the tree,
the LORD God called to the man and asked him,
"Where are you?"
—GENESIS 3:9

God, who is all knowing, all powerful, creator of all that is
living, doesn't know where Adam is? Adam has disobeyed
God and is hiding, and God can't find him? This is a twist on
the theme that God is always with us. Apparently, if we don't
want God to be with us, then we can hide, and it works.
Now, listen to God's messenger: *Hail, Mary, full of grace, the*
Lord is with you. Mary wanted God to be with her, and she hid
nothing from him—not her confusion, not her humility, not
her very self. Lord, help me be like her: knowing myself and
not hiding what I know.

Genesis 3:9–15,20
Psalm 98:1,2–3ab,3cd–4
Ephesians 1:3–6,11–12
Luke 1:26–38

DECEMBER 9

The afflicted and the needy seek water in vain,
their tongues are parched with thirst.
I, the LORD, will answer them;
I, the God of Israel, will not forsake them.
—ISAIAH 41:17

I live in Michigan, bordered by the largest freshwater lake by surface area in the world: Lake Superior. I love to gaze at water, to swim in it, to steer a boat across it, and to walk on its frozen surface. The rain on my face doesn't bother me, thunderstorms thrill me, and water in the form of snow delights me. When we have fourteen days straight without precipitation, I get anxious. This verse from Isaiah both afflicts and reassures. I feel my absolute need of God when I read it.

Isaiah 41:13–20
Psalm 145:1 and 9,10–11,12–13ab
Matthew 11:11–15

DECEMBER 10

"But wisdom is vindicated by her works."
—MATTHEW 11:19

With all the media platforms available for people to express themselves, it is often confusing to determine what are informed opinions and what is just blather. In this verse, Jesus assumes that wisdom has actual works to show. This says to me not to bother listening to a bunch of talk from others if they have no good works to back it up.

Isaiah 48:17–19
Psalm 1:1–2,3,4 and 6
Matthew 11:16–19

DECEMBER 11

• ST. DAMASUS I, POPE •

The disciples asked Jesus,
"Why do the scribes say that Elijah must come first?"
He said in reply, "Elijah will indeed come
and restore all things;
but I tell you that Elijah has already come,
and they did not recognize him but did to him
whatever they pleased."
—MATTHEW 17:10,11,12A

Driving through the Midwest, we see phenomena that appear along the roadside on a regular basis: signboard warnings of the second coming of Christ. I believe in the Second Coming, but these signs make him sound scary. In the Gospels, Jesus heals people, feeds them, forgives, and enjoys children and the poor—he's not scary. The religious people in Jesus' day did not recognize Elijah in John the Baptist. I wonder if I will recognize Jesus? What matters, I suppose, is that Jesus recognizes me.

Sirach 48:1–4,9–11
Psalm 80:2ac and 3b,15–16,18–19
Matthew 17:9a,10–13

DECEMBER 12

• THIRD SUNDAY OF ADVENT •

Have no anxiety at all, but in everything,
by prayer and petition, with thanksgiving,
make your requests known to God.
Then the peace of God that surpasses all understanding
will guard your hearts and minds in Christ Jesus.
—PHILIPPIANS 4:6–7

We pray for peace. We plead with God to relieve us of our worries. Yet little changes. War continues; discord, suspicion, prejudice, injustice, and anger fill the world. Everything we are worrying about remains and increases, and our anxiety increases, too.

But read these words: *Have no anxiety at all.* Paul tells us to pray and be thankful and let God know what we need. Then, then, then, only then, will the peace of God guard our hearts and minds. Give God peace, and your peace will return to you. Give others your peace, and your peace will return to you.

Zephaniah 3:14–18a
Isaiah 12:2–3,4,5–6(6)
Philippians 4:4–7
Luke 3:10–18

He guides the humble to justice,
he teaches the humble his way.
—PSALM 25:9

Wouldn't it be startling to read a want-ad job description that says something like this: *Seeking qualified person with either no experience or decades of experience who exhibits humility and is willing to be guided.* This is basically who God is seeking.

Numbers 24:2–7,15–17a
Psalm 25:4–5ab,6 and 7bc,8–9
Matthew 21:23–27

> *But I will leave as a remnant in your midst*
> *a people humble and lowly,*
> *Who shall take refuge in the name of the LORD:*
> *the remnant of Israel.*
> *They shall do no wrong*
> *and speak no lies;*
> *Nor shall there be found in their mouths*
> *a deceitful tongue.*
> —ZEPHANIAH 3:9,12–13A

I hear and read from some fellow Christians a wistfulness about a "remnant church." They do not seem to be afraid of a severe reduction in numbers of adherents to the faith, but rather, they long for a smaller, more pure community. Do we no longer want the tax collectors and the prostitutes? Will we excommunicate deserters who act like the apostles? If sinners have no place in the church, to whom shall we go?

Zephaniah 3:1–2,9–13
Psalm 34:2–3,6–7,17–18,19 and 23
Matthew 21:28–32

I am the LORD, there is no other;
I form the light, and create the darkness,
I make well-being and create woe;
I, the LORD, do all these things.
—ISAIAH 45:6C–7

In Genesis we read that God created people in his own image: male and female, he created them. At that point in the Bible, we don't know much about God, so being made in God's image is still obscure. We know God is a creator. And we know God is both male and female. Here, in this verse from Isaiah, we learn that God creates both light and darkness, well-being and woe. We are made in God's image so we, also, create light and darkness, well-being and woe. We do these things to ourselves and to one another. We are more powerful than we think.

Isaiah 45:6c–8,18,21c–25
Psalm 85:9ab and 10,11–12,13–14
Luke 7:18b–23

Though the mountains leave their place
and the hills be shaken,
My love shall never leave you
nor my covenant of peace be shaken,
says the LORD, who has mercy on you.
—ISAIAH 54:10

This is an extravagant metaphor—mountains moving and hills shaking—to illustrate how much mercy God offers us. We have an exuberant God, and this is a fabulous way of saying, "I love you."

Isaiah 54:1–10
Psalm 30:2 and 4,5–6,11–12a and 13b
Luke 7:24–30

May his name be blessed forever;
as long as the sun his name shall remain.
In him shall all the tribes of the earth be blessed;
all the nations shall proclaim his happiness.
—PSALM 72:17

All the nations shall proclaim his happiness. An earlier edition
reads, "may all the nations regard him as favored." The Bible
is a wondrous book inspired by the Holy Spirit, but
translations are nuanced. I recall the first time I went to Mass
in Spain and realized that the people spoke to God in the
familiar *tu* form rather than the formal *usted*. Normally, they
used "tu" only with young children, family, or good friends.
The Spanish liturgy is written as if God is a member of the
family. How wonderful!

Genesis 49:2,8–10
Psalm 72:1–2,3–4ab,7–8,17
Matthew 1:1–17

DECEMBER 18

Blessed be the LORD, the God of Israel,
who alone does wondrous deeds.
And blessed forever be his glorious name;
may the whole earth be filled with his glory.
—PSALM 72:18–19

You and I do not do wondrous deeds. Kings, presidents, doctors, philanthropists, and scientists do not do wondrous deeds either. God, alone, does wonders. We lose the sense of wonder when we think that we ourselves can accomplish it. No. Walk around today with wonder in your heart, and you may begin to regain sight. Look at individual snowflakes. Watch the clouds as they form and move. Sit by the running stream or the frozen pond. Listen to a child speak or babble.

Feel the softness of lettuce, the warmth of fire, and the slipperiness of your own wet skin. Then let your deeds, good or bad, flow into God's hands and rejoice at what he does with them.

Jeremiah 23:5–8
Psalm 72:1–2,12–13,18–19
Matthew 1:18–25

Sunday

DECEMBER 19

• FOURTH SUNDAY OF ADVENT •

"Blessed are you who believed
that what was spoken to you by the Lord
would be fulfilled."
—LUKE 1:45

Do I believe what is spoken to me by the Lord? Sort of. The Lord speaks through the Gospels, and I believe these words, but I usually assume that God is speaking to the crowd and doesn't mean every jot to apply to me. The Lord often speaks to me through the words of those in need whom I visit as part of the Society of St. Vincent de Paul. I've written entire books about what God has taught me through them. Even so, it seems impossible that God is speaking to only me. When God speaks, I picture myself in the back row of the room, listening, taking notes, but not expecting to be called on. Mary was called on. Our faith says, "Believe God speaks to you. Be like her."

Micah 5:1–4a
Psalm 80:2–3,15–16,18–19(4)
Hebrews 10:5–10
Luke 1:39–45

And coming to her, he said,
"Hail, full of grace! The Lord is with you."
But she was greatly troubled at what was said
and pondered what sort of greeting this might be.
—LUKE 1:28–29

Where did St. Luke get the details about the Annunciation?
It had to be from Mary. I picture Luke sitting down with the
Blessed Mother a long time after Jesus has ascended and the
apostles have scattered and what happened to St. Paul has
already occurred. Luke takes up a scroll and asks Mary what
she recalls about how it all began. She says, "Well, there was
this angel, and he told me the Lord was with me, and I
thought, *Who, me?* And the angel smiled and tried to prepare
me. Of course, he couldn't possibly, but I remember he
ordered me not to be afraid. So, I hung on to that." I hang on
to that, too.

Isaiah 7:10–14
Psalm 24:1–2,3–4ab,5–6
Luke 1:26–38

DECEMBER 21

• ST. PETER CANISIUS, PRIEST AND DOCTOR OF THE CHURCH •

Sing to him a new song;
pluck the strings skillfully, with shouts of gladness.
—PSALM 33:3

I like the old songs. It is comfortable to open the hymnal and say to myself, "I know this one." If the choir director introduces a new song, I listen for a couple of verses before I join in, and then only for the chorus. I don't read music, so I have to learn everything by ear. If my husband starts singing the harmony (which he does often), I am lost. Today, the psalmist encourages us to sing a new song to God. I am tempted to wait until everyone else is singing confidently before trying it myself. The spiritual life can be stunted this way: Wait and listen; make sure the others will drown out my mistakes. It's courageous to shout out loud: there is a baby born in a stable—come see!

Song of Songs 2:8–14 or Zephaniah 3:14–18a
Psalm 33:2–3,11–12,20–21
Luke 1:39–45

DECEMBER 22

Hannah, his mother, approached Eli and said: . . .
"I prayed for this child, and the LORD granted my request.
Now I, in turn, give him to the LORD;
as long as he lives, he will be dedicated to the LORD."
—1 SAMUEL 1:26A,27,28A

I was walking through a park, praying, "Jesus, what should I work on in myself? Where do I need to change?" Within a few steps I saw a paper lying flat on top of a sewer grate. It is my habit to pick up trash and toss it in the nearest receptacle, so I leaned down for it. I noticed that it was perfectly dry, clean, and flat. It was from a child's coloring book: a princess who was thoroughly doused with crayon colors. In childish scrawl were the words *Let it go!* I smiled at Jesus' quick answer. Hannah was good at it. I need to work on it, especially at Christmastime.

1 Samuel 1:24–28
1 Samuel 2:1,4–5,6–7,8abcd
Luke 1:46–56

When they came on the eighth day to circumcise
the child,
they were going to call him Zechariah
after his father,
but his mother said in reply,
"No. He will be called John."
But they answered her,
"There is no one among your relatives
who has this name."
So they made signs, asking his father what he wished
him to be called.
He asked for a tablet and wrote, "John is his name,"
and all were amazed.
—LUKE 1:59–63

What kinds of friends were these who refused to listen to
Elizabeth? Zechariah refused to listen to the angel, but he
redeemed his mistake by listening to his wife. This is one of
my favorite spiritual stories.

Malachi 3:1–4,23–24
Psalm 25:4–5ab,8–9,10 and 14
Luke 1:57–66

> *But that night the LORD spoke to Nathan and said:*
> *"Go, tell my servant David, 'Thus says the LORD:*
> *Should you build me a house to dwell in?'"*
> —2 SAMUEL 7:4–5

December 24 is a super-busy day for any mother or father.
This story from 2 Samuel is about God telling David that he
doesn't want him to build a temple. This is in sharp contrast
to the readings from tonight when the Son of David is born
in a cow stall. God wants us to build him not a home of stone
but one made of trusting hearts like Mary's and Joseph's.
Maybe the tinsel, the wrapping, and the baking are building
a stone temple, and maybe not. It depends on the softness of
my heart.

2 Samuel 7:1–5,8b–12,14a,16
Psalm 89:2–3,4–5,27 and 29
Luke 1:67–79

DECEMBER 25

The Word became flesh
and made his dwelling among us.
—JOHN 1:14A

The Word dwells among us yet. He did not die a second death. He is still here. He is alive. Where? You may find him in a stable, or fleeing across the border to a safe place, or making wine, or healing the sick, or preaching the love of God, or eating with sinners, or forgiving people, or walking on stormy seas, or feeding the hungry, or being beaten, or facing a corrupt court, or weeping, or walking in the garden. The Word dwells among us yet. He is alive. Merry Christmas!

VIGIL:
Isaiah 62:1–5
Psalm 89:4–5,16–17,27,29(2a)
Acts 13:16–17,22–25
Matthew 1:1–25 or 1:18–25

DAWN:
Isaiah 62:11–12
Psalm 97:1,6,11–12
Titus 3:4–7
Luke 2:15–20

NIGHT:
Isaiah 9:1–6
Psalm 96:1–2,2–3,11–12,13
Titus 2:11–14
Luke 2:1–14

DAY:
Isaiah 52:7–10
Psalm 98:1,2–3,3–4,5–6(3c)
Hebrews 1:1–6
John 1:1–18 or 1:1–5,9–14

DECEMBER 26

"When his parents saw him,
they were astonished,
and his mother said to him,
'Son, why have you done this to us?
Your father and I have been looking for you
with great anxiety.'"
—LUKE 2:48

We don't get exactly what we ask for on Christmas. It's the same with family: we don't get perfect parents, or perfect siblings, or perfect children. Mary and Joseph actually got a perfect child, but in this story he gave them a gift card instead of the cash they would have preferred. Jesus gives each of us a gift card instead of cash for Christmas. Today, take that gift card, ponder it, and then pick out something from the shop that you can share with others.

1 Samuel 1:20–22,24–28 or Sirach 3:2–6,12–14
Psalm 84:2–3,5–6,9–10 or Psalm 128:1–2,3,4–5
1 John 3:1–2,21–24 or Colossians 3:12–21 or 3:12–17
Luke 2:41–52

Beloved:
What was from the beginning,
what we have heard,
what we have seen with our eyes,
what we looked upon
and touched with our hands
concerns the Word of life—
for the life was made visible;
we have seen it and testify to it.
—1 JOHN 1:1–2A

John heard, saw, and touched Jesus. His testimony is full of first-hand experiences. Once, while making a phone call to a business, I was told, "Please hold." And then, "You may hear silence until your call is answered." I'm glad they told me because I expect music on hold, so, when the silence ensued, I might have thought the call had been dropped. John tells us what he heard. Relax in the silence.

1 John 1:1–4
Psalm 97:1–2,5–6,11–12
John 20:1a and 2–8

DECEMBER 28

• THE HOLY INNOCENTS, MARTYRS •

This is the message that we have heard from Jesus Christ
and proclaim to you:
God is light, and in him there is no darkness at all.
—1 JOHN 1:5

Picture the most beautiful light you can imagine: shimmering
beams reaching to earth through huge cumulous clouds, or
sparkling snow on a mountain, or moving sunlight on a
glittering summer sea. Now, picture the story of the Holy
Innocents: screams of parents; wails of siblings; limp, bloody
bodies of babies. God is light. The darkness is not part of
God. But God is always with us. God is the light in the
darkness. God is the moon in the night sky. God is the
tenderness of love. God is the compassion in our mourning.
God is the peace after chaos. God did not will the death of
the Holy Innocents. God caught their souls in his arms and
surrounded them in light forever.

1 John 1:5—2:2
Psalm 124:2–3,4–5,7b–8
Matthew 2:13–18

The child's father and mother were amazed
at what was said about him;
and Simeon blessed them and said to Mary,
his mother,
"Behold, this child is destined
for the fall and rise of many in Israel,
and to be a sign that will be contradicted."
—LUKE 2:33–34

Simeon, the devout and righteous man, recognized the Messiah disguised as a newborn baby. How many little babies and children there must have been in Jerusalem, yet this one caught his attention. Simeon praised and thanked God, and then he blessed the young parents. We never see Simeon in the Gospels again. His job was to recognize that God had visited his people and to speak up with praise and blessing. This Christmas season, remember Simeon's story. His simple response is what God asks of us.

1 John 2:3–11
Psalm 96:1–2a,2b–3,5b–6
Luke 2:22–35

DECEMBER 30

There was a prophetess, Anna,
the daughter of Phanuel, of the tribe of Asher.
—LUKE 2:36

I notice that many of the people in the Gospel stories do not
have names: the blind man, the lepers, the woman at the
well, the centurion, the scribes and Pharisees. Even some of
the apostles are given simple descriptions and single names.
But Anna is described by what she does (a prophetess), by
her father (Phanuel), and even by her tribe (Asher). We learn
how long she was married and how she lived her life as a
widow. Are you a simple churchgoer? Do you live alone?
Does your life consist of prayer, fasting, and worship? You
are more important than you think. God sees your
faithfulness. He sends his Son to you. He remembers your
name and all about you. Your life, like Anna's, is written in
his book.

1 John 2:12–17
Psalm 96:7–8a,8b–9,10
Luke 2:36–40

DECEMBER 31

In the beginning was the Word,
and the Word was with God,
and the Word was God.
—JOHN 1:1

The Word was God. God is love. God is full of grace and truth. God is the light. Repeat these phrases slowly to yourself. Whisper them to your soul. Do it as often as you need to be reminded that your soul belongs to God. Your soul is with God. God's grace, truth, and light shine in and through you. You were made by love, for love. Nothing can separate you from any of this except your own decision to step away. Stay close, and may God bless you always. Amen. Alleluia.

1 John 2:18–21
Psalm 96:1–2,11–12,13
John 1:1–18

ABOUT THE AUTHOR

Jane Knuth is a longtime volunteer in the Society of St. Vincent de Paul in Kalamazoo, Michigan. Her first book, *Thrift Store Saints*, was awarded first place from the Catholic Press Association for Popular Presentation of the Catholic Faith. Jane is the author of *Thrift Store Graces*, *Love Will Steer Me True* (coauthored with her daughter Ellen Knuth), and *The Prayer List*. She also writes a monthly column for *The Good News*, the newspaper of the Diocese of Kalamazoo.

Also by **JANE KNUTH**

Thrift Store Saints
Meeting Jesus 25¢ at a Time

In this collection of true stories based on
Jane Knuth's experience serving the poor
at a St. Vincent de Paul thrift store, readers
will discover the profound joy any of us can
experience when serving those in need.

PB | 978-0-8294-3301-2 | $13.95

Thrift Store Graces
Finding God's Gifts in the
Midst of the Mess

In her follow-up to *Thrift Store Saints*, Knuth
introduces readers to challenging personal
situations that emerge as a result of her
volunteer work. This witty and inspiring
book will compel readers to rethink why
we serve others.

PB | 978-00-8294-3692-1 | $13.95